WHO'S WHO
IN INTERNATIONAL
WINTER
SPORTS

WHO'S WHO
IN INTERNATIONAL
WINTER
SPORTS

EDITED BY DAVID EMERY

SPHERE

SPHERE BOOKS LIMITED
30-32 Gray's Inn Road, London WC1X 8JL

Jayne Torvill and Christopher Dean

First published in Great Britain by
Sphere Books Ltd 1983
Copyright © First Editions 1983 (Rambletree
Limited) 1983

Edited, designed and produced by First Editions
(Rambletree Limited)

SPHERE

Set in Century by Jigsaw Graphics, London

Printed in Italy by New Interlitho SpA.

Introduction

The exciting world of winter sports, played against a background of dazzling white snow and ice in glamorous resorts like St. Moritz and Aspen, is also a world of talent, hard training and determination, as competitive as any other field of sport. Many different sports come under the broad heading of winter sports – but they all compete on ice or snow. Skaters specialise in figure skating, pairs skating, ice dancing or speed skating. Skiers tackle downhill racing, slalom, giant slalom, ski jumping, cross country or biathlon. And there are the bobbers . . .

The personalities involved in winter sports are as diverse as the sports themselves: some achieve international fame, like Britain's Jayne Torvill and Christopher Dean, or become national heroes like Ingemar Stenmark of Sweden; others shine brightly but briefly before burning themselves out.

Who's Who in International Winter Sports lists, in alphabetical order, all the men and women who compete in winter sports events at the highest level. In addition to current leading competitors, we have included those on their way up and others who are on the point of retiring, to give a complete reference book.

Marat Akbarov
Pairs skater
Born: February 3, 1961, Moscow,
U.S.S.R.
Height: 5–7. *Weight:* 148.
Career Highlights
World Championships: fifth 1983;
sixth 1982.
European Championships: fourth
1982, 1983.
U.S.S.R. Championships: silver
medal 1983.

See **Veronica Pershina**

Caroline Attia
Ski downhill
Born: July 4, 1960, Paris, France.
Height: 4–9. *Weight:* 101.
Career Highlights
World Championships: *downhill:* 21st,
1978.
World Cup: *overall:* 21st, 1983; 28th,
1979; *downhill:* fourth, 1983.

The performance of the little
Parisienne was one of the most surprising features of the 1983 women's
ski season. Until 1982 she had suggested little, although in season 1980-81
she had had a fourth place at Schruns
and an eighth at Val d'Isere. After
missing the next season, she
positively exploded in December
1982 at Sansicario in Italy. It was one
of those races where the track seems
to quicken and the late numbers on
the start list came powering in . . . led
by Attia. She held her form with a
third place in the next race at
Schruns.

Sabine Baess
Pairs skater
Born: March 15, 1961, Karl-Marx-
Stadt, East Germany.

Height: 5–0. *Weight:* 86.
Career Highlights
Olympic Games: sixth 1980.
World Championships: gold medal
1982; silver 1983.
European Championships: gold
medal 1982, 1983.
East German Championships: gold
medal 1983.

It seemed after the 1982 World
Championships that Sabine Baess
and her partner Tassilo Thierbach,
trained by Irene Salzmann, might
have a long reign. They won the free
skating and were second in the short
programme.Although they took their
own national championships in 1983,
they went to Dortmund to defend
their European title – the girl who
likes needlework and cooking, and the
boy who likes motor sport – with a
problem. She had injured her back
just before Christmas and they didn't
know until a month before Dortmund
if they would be able to skate at all.

They were good enough to retain
the title, but it was by no means a con-
vincing performance: at one point the
French judge marked another East
German pair, Birgit Lorenz and Knut
Schubert, above them, while a
Russian judge preferred Veronica
Pershina and Marat Akbarov. Even
so, they took the short programme
and the free and went off to Helsinki
for the World Championships, where
they took the short again. But the
Russians Valova and Vasiliev – snap-
ping at their heels after the short programme – won the free skating and
the gold medal.

Karen Barber
Ice dancer
Born: June 21, 1961, Manchester,
England.

Sabine Baess and Tassilo Thierbach.

Height: 5–2.   *Weight:* 103.
Career Highlights
World Championships: fifth 1983;
  seventh 1982.
European Championships: bronze
  medal 1983; fifth 1981, 1982.
British Championships: silver medal
  1978, 1979, 1980, 1981, 1982.
St. Ivel: second 1982.
N.H.K. Trophy: winner 1981.
Ennia Challenge Cup: winner 1982.

To live in the shadows of Torvill and Dean can't be easy, but so far Karen Barber and Nicky Slater have managed it – smiling. They met in Manchester where, going from the rink on a bus, he asked her to skate with him and she promptly refused. (She surrendered gracefully a little while later).

Their career has had its problems, at one stage financial, although that has passed now and they are determined to go on beyond the 1984 Winter Olympic Games. They train with Jimmy Young at Richmond, although this involves starting after midnight on occasion, when the ice is clear of other skaters. They both manage to do 25 hours a week. Hardship seems to have fashioned a good temperament as well as pure determination. At the European Championships in 1981, they were fifth throughout. That was the year they won the N.H.K. Trophy and even a week later Karen had the biggest grin you could imagine. In 1982 at the Europeans, they were again fifth all the way through, but in the Worlds at Copenhagen, where the Americans

Karen Barber and Nicky Slater.

came in, they were down to seventh.

When Jayne Torvill had to miss the 1983 Europeans through injury, we wondered . . . had Slater and Barber's great moment arrived? They'd spent some time before training at Garmisch and now journeyed to Dortmund. They were in second place after the compulsory dances and original set pattern, but were eventually beaten back by Soviets Volozhinskaya and Svinin and were happy to have the bronze medal.

It maintained a remarkable sequence. Britain has won a medal of some sort in every European, World and Olympic event since 1976.

At the 1983 World Championships in Helsinki they were fourth after the compulsory dances, eighth in the original set pattern and fifth in the free dancing for an overall fifth – two places up on the year before.

Konrad Bartelski
Ski downhill
Born: May 27, 1954, Holland.
Height: 5–11.   *Weight:* 177.
Career Highlights
Olympic Games: *downhill:* 12th, 1980.
World Championships: *downhill:*
  15th, 1974; 16th, 1982; 17th, 1978.
World Cup: second in downhill event
  at Val Gardena, December, 1981.

For a decade, Konrad Bartelski waged a difficult and sometimes lonely struggle against the odds. The son of a Polish father and English mother, Bartelski's career stretches back to 1974, when he was one of a group who organised the British Alpine team and got it onto a proper footing, no matter that they could never have the backing, facilities or sheer numbers of the Alpine nations they set out to beat.

Konrad Bartelski.

At Megeve in 1975 Bartelski fell so hard he was taken to hospital unconscious by helicopter. This spectacular crash made him famous in Europe, if not in Britain, where ski racing is enormously popular on television. Customs officers would stop him and say: *'Aren't you the man who had that crash?'.*

At Lake Placid in the 1980 Olympics he was 12th in the downhill. It was easily the best result ever by a British man and it might have been the moment for him to end his career. But he stayed . . . to enjoy a greater moment. In the second World Cup race of 1981-82 – at Val Gardena – his start number was 29th, right back in the wilderness. The big names had long gone and the fastest of them,

Erwin Resch, was already being feted as the winner. This is standard practice in ski races: outsiders from 29th just don't win. Bartelski had a cold, but he went down all the same. At the first point on the course where times are taken, he was faster than Resch and he held that to the second point. The exact margin in his favour .22 of a second.

His time at the end was 2 mins. 7.52 secs – nine hundredths slower than Resch. But he was second, a result straight from the improbable, not to say unbelievable. It set the tone for a very good season: 15th at Crans-Montana, 13th at Garmisch, 15th at Aspen, 16th in the World Championship at Schladming. These results must be seen in context: he is not a member of a powerful team with truck-loads of technical personnel and big budgets, he is in a sense an outsider.

In 1983, he had a poor season falling here and there. It was like watching a loop of an old film. But what was worse, he didn't ever look as if he was going to master the mountains again. He announced his retirement at Lake Louise, Canada, at the end of the season.

Gary Beacom
Singles figure skater
Born: February 23, 1960, Don Mills, Ontario, Canada.
Height: 5–9. *Weight:* 145.
Career Highlights
World Championships: 13th 1983.
Canadian Championships: silver medal 1983; bronze 1980; fourth 1981; fifth 1982.
Skate Moscow: fifth 1982.
Skate America: eighth 1981.

Known for his compulsory figures – he was 11th in them at the 1983 World Championships – Beacom is a full time university student reading philosophy and physics (most unusual in a skater). However, he manages to train for 35 hours a week in the summer and 25 in the winter. As his results show, he's had a varied career in the Canadian Championships despite his innovative free skating.

When he has time, he enjoys running, cycling, tennis and making wall hangings. He skated in the 1983 World Championships and was 13th overall. His home club is the Toronto Cricket, Skating and Curling Club, though he has yet to be known to play cricket.

Pierre Bechu
Ice dancer
Born: March 10, 1959, Bron, France.
Height: 5–8. *Weight:* 148.
Career Highlights
World Championships: 11th 1982.
European Championships: fifth 1983; sixth 1981, 1982.
St. Gervais: second 1981.
Morzine: second 1982.

See **Nathalie Herve**

Martin Bell
Ski downhill
Born: December 6, 1964, Edinburgh, Scotland.
Height: 5–9. *Weight:* 176.
Career Highlights
World Cup: *overall:* 77th 1983.

Very much the second member of Britain's team behind Konrad Bartelski, Bell suffered cruel misfortune when he ruptured the ligaments in his left leg just before the 1981/82 season, and then missed most of the next season due to another injury. He's a strong downhiller and regarded as extremely promising.

In 1983 he was 45th at Pontresina – starting impossibly far back at 77 –44th at Val Gardena, starting 82nd in one race and 38th in the next. He missed the middle of the season because of the shoulder. He was 53rd at St. Anton, 24th at Aspen – again improving his start position dramatically (it was 55th) – and 38th at Lake Louise.

Born: January 6, 1960, Moscow, U.S.S.R.
Height: 5–5. *Weight:* 112.
Career Highlights
Olympic Games: eighth 1980.
World Championships: silver medal 1982, 1983; bronze medal 1981.
European Championships: gold medal 1983; silver 1982; fourth 1981.
U.S.S.R. Championships: gold medal 1983.

Natalia Bestemianova
Ice dancer

Natalia Bestemianova and Andrei Bukin.

With Andrei Bukin, Natalia Bestemianova represents the main threat to Britain's Torvill and Dean for an Olympic gold medal. He is the quiet one, she bubbles with life and says: '*I like the feeling of being happy.*'

She lives in a small town called Shertabovo, where she runs in the lonely forests as part of her fitness programme – and she does need to be fit. She explodes on the ice (somebody said that for every minute in the day, Natalia lives two). '*I do get nervous, but I don't want people to see that,*' she says – nervous because their skating is so full of risks. Their programmes are created to complement her personality. Bukin, married to his first partner Olga Abalkina, is not only quiet but strong and sure – and Natalia needs that.

At the European Championships at Innsbruck in 1981, the Russian couple were fourth – and they were only beginning their serious assault. A year later, at Lyons, they were up to second place, but that was when Torvill and Dean started to get marks of 6.0 all over the place. The Russians were achieving 5.9s and it wasn't enough.

A great deal changed in 1983. Torvill and Dean missed the European Championships because Jayne Torvill was injured, and the Russians grabbed their chance. They won all three sections – compulsory dances, original set pattern and free dance –although they were criticised afterwards by former champions Angelika and Erich Buck who said: '*Eighty per cent of what they do could be done off the ice without skates. It may be dancing, but it is not ice dancing.*'

Torvill and Dean were back for the World Championshps in Helsinki, and the Russians back in second place again (third in the compulsories, third in the original set pattern and second in the free). She enjoys music and the theatre; he enjoys motor sports.

Judy Blumberg
Ice dancer
Born: September 13th, 1957, Santa Monica, California, U.S.A.
Height: 5–3. *Weight:* 106.
Career Highlights
Olympic Games: seventh 1980.
World Championships: bronze medal 1983; fourth 1981, 1982.
U.S.A. Championships: gold medal 1981, 1982, 1983; silver 1980.
Skate Canada: winner 1980.

There is a three-way national struggle for supremacy in ice dancing, no matter that Torvill and Dean are so far in front of everybody else. At world level, taking Helsinki 1983 as a form guide, only one couple in the top eight were not from Britain, the Soviet Union or the United States. Judy Blumberg and Michael Seibert represent the hopes of America, and they are ever closer to getting in front of all the Soviets . . . second only to Torvill and Dean after the first two sections of competition at Helsinki, but then back to third in the final analysis.

The American couple can be extremely elegant. Interestingly they have been training at Richmond, Surrey, with an Englishman, Bobby Thompson. In this year's U.S.A. Championships Seibert said; '*We've worked very hard on the compulsories. I think we're skating a hundred per cent better than last year.*' Although Blumberg tripped in the free dancing, they were given an astonishing five marks of 6.0. A measure of their improvement came at Helsinki, though they couldn't get the silver medal from Soviet couple Bestemianova and Bukin, even though Bestemianova made mistakes. Their duel, due to be resumed in Olympic year, should be fascinating.

She likes ski-ing, cooking, working with animals and youngsters; he likes painting and costume design.

Judy Blumberg and Michael Seibert.

Hristina Boianova
Ice dancer
Born: February 11, 1966, Sofia,
  Bulgaria.
Height: 5–2. *Weight:* 103.
Career Highlights
Bulgarian Championships: gold medal
  1981, 1982.

The beautiful red-headed Hristina and
her partner Iavor Ivanov prove that
sport is about taking part as well as
winning. Despite the fact that they are
coached by Viktor Rizhkin, who was
once the famous Ludmila Pakhomova's
first partner, they set a macabre sort of
record in 1983. In the European Championships at Dortmund, they were 17th
of 17, and last in all three sections. In
the World Championships at Helsinki
they were 18th of 18 although actually
19th of 19 in the compulsory dances
before French couple Nathalie Herve
and Pierre Bechu retired through illness. It means that everybody has
beaten them at everything. But . . .
somebody has to be last, haven't they?
And since Bulgaria has no known tradition of ice dancing, it's good to see
them taking part.

For the record, they train 12 hours a
week in summer and 18 in winter,
about half the recognised work load.
She likes jazz and he likes
choreography.

Brian Boitano
Singles figure skater
Born: October 22, 1963, Sunnyvale,
  California, U.S.A.
Height: 5–11. *Weight:* 148.
Career Highlights
World Championships: seventh 1983.
United States Championships: silver
  medal 1983; fourth 1982.
Skate Canada: winner 1982.
Ennia Challenge Cup: winner 1982.

This brown haired, hazel-eyed Californian made a good debut in the 1983
World Championships. He's been moving up since he was second in the
Pacific Coast Championships in 1980:
he won it the next year and has held it
since. His strengths are his triple Lutz
with his arms over his head and his triple Axel combination.

In 1982 he achieved two
breakthroughs, winning the Ennia
Challenge Cup at the Hague in November – he took both the short programme and the free – from such
established skaters as Norbert
Schramm, Josef Sabovcik and Igor
Bobrin; and he won Skate Canada in
October – first in the compulsory
figures, second in the short, second in
the free – against Brian Orser and
Heiko Fischer.

In the 1983 World Championships
in Helsinki, he was ninth after the compulsory figures, seventh in the short
programme and sixth in the free skating. His hobbies are bike riding and
drawing.

Petra Born
Ice dancer
Born: August 1, 1965, Zweibrucken,
  West Germany.
Height: 5–4. *Weight:* 115.
Career Highlights
World Championships: ninth 1983;
  14th 1982; 21st 1981.
European Championships: sixth 1983;
  11th 1982; 16th 1981.
West German Championships: gold
  medal 1983; silver medal 1982.

With her partner Rainer Schonborn
(who's been skating since 1970), Petra
has been making steady progress. They
were held in second place in their
national championships in 1982 by
Peter Klisch and Birgit Goller – as in

1981 – but duly became champions in 1983, when Klisch and Goller had retired.

Interestingly, Betty Callaway –coach of Torvill and Dean – has been helping them and they say with disarming candour that their progress has been speeded up by training at Obertsdorf, where they can follow the dance patterns of the British couple. (They are actually trained by Martin Skotnicky). Mrs. Callaway was in Dortmund in 1983 to watch them in the European Championships, where they were sixth.

The improvement was maintained in the 1983 World Championships in Helsinki where they got into the top ten for the first time – tenth in the compulsory dances, ninth in the original set pattern and ninth in the free dancing. They train 24 hours a week in summer, 18 in winter. She likes reading, dancing and riding; he likes swimming and dancing.

Todd Brooker.

Todd Brooker
Ski downhill
Born: November 24, 1959, Paris, Ontario, Canada.
Height: 6–0.   *Weight:* 198.
Career Highlights
World Championships: *downhill:* 13th, 1982.
World Cup: *overall:* 27th, 1983; *downhill:* ninth, 1983.

The latest of the Canadian downhillers started the 1982 season quietly – 14th at Val Gardena, 14th at Crans Montana, 13th at Kitzbuehel, 15th at Garmisch. But when the circuit moved to North America he suddenly thrust himself to the forefront: fifth at Mount Whistler, ninth in the first race at Aspen, second in another race at Aspen.

In 1983 he confirmed everything: 36th at Pontresina, sixth at Val Gardena, 17th at Kitzbuehel, and then

a moment of triumph, a victory in the second Kitzbuehel race, from Urs Raber and fellow Canadian Ken Read. He abandoned at Val d'Isere twice, was 14th at Sarajevo, 15th at St. Anton – and then won at Aspen.

He comes from an area with no ski tradition, but a two and a half hour drive north is a ski resort called Blue Mountain, which has a vertical drop of 600ft: enough to begin with.

Peter Brugnani
Bobsleigh
Born: October 28, 1958, London, England..
Height: 6–1. *Weight:* 208.
Career Highlights
British Four-man Championships: gold medal, 1983.
British Two-man Championships: gold medal, 1983.
British Brakeman's Cup: winner 1982.

See **Malcolm Lloyd**

Toni Buergler.

Toni Buergler
Ski downhill
Born: July 17, 1957, Rickenbach, Switzerland.
Height: 5–7. *Weight:* 165.
Career Highlights
World Championships: *downhill:* seventh, 1982.
World Cup: *overall:* 20th, 1979; 22nd, 1982; 24th, 1981; *downhill:* sixth, 1981.
Swiss Championships: *downhill:* gold medal, 1981.

The former bricklayer is one of the new generation of downhill racers who started in 1979 and have now reached maturity. That '79 season gave him a promising start, 20th overall in the World Cup with one tremendous result,

a first place at Crans Montana where, after the race, he could be seen spraying a bottle of champagne all around him.

He started 1982 well, third in the opening round of the World Cup in Val d'Isere, but it was to be his best result. In the World Championships downhill he was seventh. In 1983, he was ninth at Pontresina, 14th at Val d'Isere and tenth at St. Anton.

Andrei Bukin
Ice dancer
Born: June 10, 1957, Moscow, U.S.S.R.
Height: 6–0. *Weight:* 135.
Career Highlights
Olympic Games: eighth 1980.
World Championships: silver medal 1982, 1983; bronze medal 1981.

European Championships: gold medal 1983; silver 1982; fourth 1981.
U.S.S.R. Championships: gold medal 1983.

See **Natalia Bestemianova**

Horst Bulau
Ski jumper
Born: August 14, 1962, Ottawa, Canada.
Height: 5–6.   *Weight:* 142.
Career Highlights
Junior World Championships: gold medal, 1979.
World Cup: second, 1981, 1982, 1983.
Canadian Junior Championships: gold medal, 1978.

Bulau is a scratch golfer as well as a talented ski jumper – his sister ski jumps, too. Brent Rushall, a Canadian professor who specialises in sport psychology, says that Bulau has what it takes to be a world champion. He is a natural athlete ,too, like Finn Matti Nykaenen.

He fell during the World Championships in Harrachow and had bad concussion, and came to Planica and the culmination of the season needing to win both the 70 and 90 metre jumps – with Nykaenen coming no higher than third – to be world champion. Nykaenen promptly won the 70 metres and that was that. Nykaenen said: *'I think Bulau is the second best ski jumper in the world.'* He is also a strong and determined man – what one West German described as tough in the nicest sense.

Michel Canac
Ski slalom
Born: August 2, 1956, Aime, France.
Height: 5–4.   *Weight:* 141.

Career Highlights
World Cup: *overall:* 31st, 1983; *slalom:* 11th, 1983.

In a short space of time – barely two seasons – Canac, who sports an impressive moustache, has set out to redeem his country in the slalom, his speciality. In 1982, he was in the top 15 twice – at Wengen (12th) and Montgenevre (15th).

1983 didn't start well when he abandoned in the second run at Courmayeur. But he was ninth at Madonna, and into the top ten for the first time. He was seventh at Parpan, ninth at Kitzbuehel, and third at Kranjska Gora, beaten only by Franz Gruber and Stig Strand. He abandoned in the second run at Markstein, but was fourth at St. Anton five days later. The 'white circus' returned to Markstein and this time he was 13th. He rounded off the season with a seventh place at Furano.

Sandra Cariboni
Singles figure skater
Born: November 17, 1963, Zofingen, Switzerland.
Height: 5–6.   *Weight:* 127.
Career Highlights
World Championships: tenth 1983; 16th 1982.
European Championships: 13th 1982, 1983.
Swiss Championships: gold medal 1983; silver medal 1982.

If versatility won gold medals, Cariboni, who has skated since 1972, would win plenty. She can ski, enjoys jazz, ballet, painting, fashion and knitting. She was second in the Swiss Championships in 1982 and so comparatively unknown that one periodical referred to her as Sandra Caribone.

Peter and Caitlin Carruthers.

These things will happen, but not for long.

In the European Championships that year – Lyons – she was 13th in the compulsory figures, 14th in the short programme and 15th in the free skating. She won the Swiss Championship in 1983 and went off to the Europeans at Dortmund still finding her way, although she was third in the compulsory figures and actually second in one of them (the loops). She collapsed dramatically to 19th in the short programme and was 16th in the free. But she improved clearly in the World Championships a month later – fourth in the figures, always a good springboard, 16th in the short, and 12th in the free for an overall tenth place.

She skates 25 hours a week in summer and between 20 and 25 hours a week in winter.

Caitlin Carruthers
Pairs skater
Born: May 30, 1961, Boston, Massachusetts, U.S.A.
Height: 5–0. *Weight:* 93.
Career Highlights
Olympic Games: fifth 1980.
World Championships: bronze medal 1982; fourth 1983.
United States Championships: gold medal 1981, 1982, 1983.
N.H.K. Trophy: winner 1981.
Skate America: second 1981.
Ennia Challenge Cup: second 1981.

Caitlin and Peter Carruthers, the brother and sister from Boston –now members of the Skating Club of Wilmington, Delaware – have dominated U.S. pairs skating since the Olympic games in 1980, but have never been good enough at international level to dislodge the Soviet or East German

leading pairs and were overtaken in the 1983 World Championships by Canadians Underhill and Martini.

The Carruthers are coached by Ron Ludington, who also helps with their choreography along with Ricky Harris. Both skaters are high school graduates and their specialist moves on the ice are the hydrant lift, the lateral twist and the throw triple Salchow.

In the 1982 World Championships in Copenhagen – they had been fifth in 1981 – they took the bronze medal one place above Underhill and Martini. In the 1983 World Championships they were a disappointing fifth in the short programme and fourth in the free skating.

He likes music and racketball; she likes music, needlework and reading.

Peter Carruthers
Pairs skater
Born: July 22, 1959, Boston, Massachussetts, U.S.A.
Height: 5–11.   *Weight:* 153.
Career Highlights
Olympic Games: fifth 1980.
World Championships: bronze medal 1982; fourth 1983.
United States Championships: gold medal 1981, 1982, 1983.
N.H.K. Trophy: winner 1981.
Skate America: second 1981.
Ennia Challenge Cup: second 1981.

See **Caitlin Carruthers**

Conradin Cathomen
Ski downhill
Born: June 2, 1959, Laax, Switzerland.
Height: 5–7.   *Weight:* 159.
Career Highlights
World Championships: *downhill:* silver medal, 1982.
World Cup: *overall:* 14th, 1983;

downhill: second, 1983.
European Junior Championships:
downhill: fourth, 1977.

The personable young man from the German speaking part of Switzerland has recently opened a sports shop, and, after his superb second place in the 1982 World Championships, there ought to be no lack of customers. Cathomen was very much one of the discoveries of that season, despite a difficult start to his career.

In 1980, he was 102 on the FIS rankings, and had to change ski companies three times. But all that improved in 1982 with a ninth place, a second and third and that World Championship silver medal in the downhill.

Cathomen won his first World Cup downhill the next season at Val Gardena, on a course softened by overnight snow, but still with hard, icy turns. He averaged 95.77 kph for a time of 2 mins. 9.54 secs. *'The course was very rough,'* he said but, because he is such a good technical racer, that did not matter at all, even over 3.45 kilometres. He was third in the final downhill of the season behind Franz Klammer.

His hobbies are cycling, hang-gliding and tennis.

Rudi Cerne
Singles figure skater
Born: September 26, 1958, Wanne-
  Eickel, West Germany.
Height: 5–10. *Weight:* 148.
Career Highlights
Olympic Games: 13th 1980.
World Championships: tenth 1983;
  13th 1980; 14th 1978; 15th 1982.
European Championships: fourth
  1982; seventh 1978, 1983.
West German Championships: gold

Rudi Cerne.

medal 1978, 1980; silver 1982; bronze 1983.

That the name of Rudi Cerne is often mentioned with, or measured against, that of John Curry is an astonishing reflection on his artistry. In terms of finishing positions he has done nothing to justify anything like that in a switch-back career, but in terms of ability he has.

Many regard his as a wasted talent. This has not prevented Cerne from delighting and perhaps astonishing audiences all over the place. For example, in the 1983 European Championships, when he was seventh, he captivated the crowd even during the warm up and afterwards said: *'I noticed that the audience liked my free programme. I liked it too'.* In fact, at the German Championships in 1982, he led after the compulsory figures, but was overtaken in the short programme and fell in the free. At the 1982 European Championships he was fourth (he was being trained by Carlo Fassi) and earned the approval of Curry himself. But his performance at the 1983 World Championships was disappointing; tenth in the compulsory figures, 11th in the short programme and eighth in the free, despite charming everyone as ever with his wonderfully expressive expertise.

Olga Charvatova
Ski racer
Born: June 11, 1962, Gottwaldov, Czechoslovakia.
Height: 5–6.   *Weight:* 149.
Career Highlights
World Championships: *downhill:* 19th, 1982; 25th, 1978; *giant slalom:* 18th, 1982; *slalom:* ninth, 1982; 22nd, 1978.
World Cup: *overall:* eight, 1983; 15th, 1981; 17th, 1979; *giant slalom:* 13th, 1983; *slalom:* 14th, 1983.

The Czech girl has been making steady progress since 1978 and 1983 was her best so far, thanks to solid performances in all three Alpine disciplines. Her 1983 highlights were: in the slalom, a sixth at Schruns and Waterville Valley; in the giant slalom, a sixth at Mont Tremblant; and in the downhill a fourth at Jahorina.

Elisabeth Chaud
Ski downhill
Born: December 7, 1960, Puy-Saint-Vincent, France.
Height: 5–2.   *Weight:* 119.
Career Highlights
World Championships: *downhill:* 16th, 1982.
World Cup: *overall:* 11th, 1982; 17th, 1983; *downhill:* sixth, 1983; eighth,

Olga Charvatova.

1982; 27th 1981; *giant slalom:* 20th, 1983.

She comes from a ski resort – Puy-Saint-Vincent and has taken only three seasons to establish her reputation. She also competes in the giant slalom and in 1983 was 20th in the World Cup.

But the downhill is her forte. She started 1983 with a disappointing 19th at Sansicario, but was second in the next race at Schruns behind Doris de Agostini and only eight hundredths of a second away from victory. She was just out of the top ten for the next three races before coming fifth at Jahorina. At Mont Tremblant in Canada, it all went wrong with a 41st place after starting ninth.

Tiffany Chin
Singles figure skater
Born: March 10, 1967, Tuluca Lake,

California, U.S.A.
Height: 4–9.   *Weight:* 89.
Career Highlights
World Championships: ninth 1983.
World Junior Championships: gold
medal 1982.
United States Championships: bronze
medal 1983; fifth 1982.
United States Junior Championships:
silver medal 1980.
Skate America: fourth 1982.
N.H.K. Trophy: third 1982.

The little girl with a face of unmistakably Oriental descent from the San Diego Figure Skating Club enjoys reading – as well as skating. She had suggested what she might be able to achieve by becoming World Junior Champion in 1982 and in Skate America, at Lake Placid in October 1982, was fourth behind leading competitors like Rosalynn Sumners, Claudia Leistner and Kristina Wegelius (seventh in the compulsory figures, sixth in the short, second in the free programme). Another competitor wrote: *'She skated an extremely good long programme, executing many triple jumps but to the crowds' surprise, she did not attempt the triple Axel which she has so successfully accomplished in practice.'*

At Pittsburg in February 1983, in the United States Championships, she improved two places from the previous year: fifth in the figures, fourth in the short programme and third in the free, with what Alex McGowan – a noted coach, bon viveur and expert judge of skating – saw as *'a breezy new programme that contained two nice triple toe loops, two fine double Axels and some excellent choreography. Her only blemish was a fall on the triple Salchow.'*

She went to the 1983 World Championships in Helsinki – her first World Championship – and did not do badly; 14th in the figures, sixth in the short,

seventh in the free for an overall ninth place.

She skates 32 hours a week and was once coached by Frank Carroll. Her present coach is John Nicks.

Steve Collins
Ski jumper
Born: March 4, 1964, Thunder Bay,
Ontario, Canada.
Height: 5–7.   *Weight:* 113.
Career Highlights
Olympic Games: 15th, 1980.
World Junior Championships: gold
medal, 1979.
World Cup: 14th, 1981.

As a 15-year-old Collins won a World Cup event in Lahti, setting a hill record of 124 metres on the 90 metre jump. A Finnish journalist – and Finns are connoisseurs of ski jumping – remarked in awe: *'I thought he would never come down.'* In a sense, Collins jumped twice: when he was halfway through the flight he felt a gust of wind coming up the hill. It lifted him and he said to himself: *'I might just as well give that a ride too.'* It was his first season on the World Cup circuit. That same year he jumped 114.5 from the 90 metre mark in the 1980 Lake Placid Olympic Games where he was the youngest competitor.

He is an Ojibwa Indian and known for his reticence. His flying style, reminiscent of Finn Matti Nykaenen, quickly earned him the nickname 'Snowflake'. But he is maturing and before the first tournament in 1983 – in Innsbruck – actually presented himself for an interview.

Cynthia Coull
Pairs skater
Born: August 14, 1965, Greenfield
Park, Quebec, Canada.

Steve Collins.

Doris de Agostini.

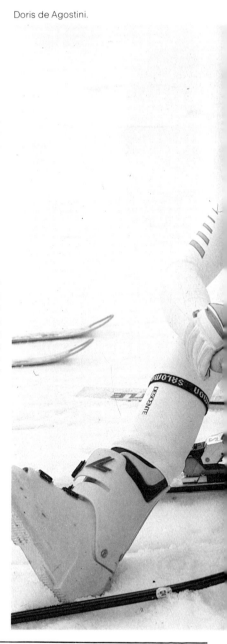

Height: 4–11.   *Weight:* 90.
Career Highlights
World Championships: ninth, 1983.
Canadian Championships: silver medal
   1983.
Skate America: fourth 1982.

The new pair of Cynthia Coull and
Mark Rowsom announced themselves
at the 1982 Skate America event when
they were a strong fourth, having landed side by side triple cherry jumps.

Coull is also a very good singles
skater (she was reserve for the Canadian team in the 1983 World Championships), and at the Canadian
Championships was third in the
women's section – tenth in the compulsory figures, third in the short programme and second in the free.

Rowsom, who has skated since
1961, began his pairs career with
another partner, Becky Gough. The
partnership of Coull and Rowsom was
established only in 1982. In that short
space of time they have learned fast
and now include all the difficult pairs
moves, including the side by side triple
toe loop and double Axel jumps.

A direct measure of their potential
came in the 1983 World Championships, when they were ninth in
both the short programme and free
skating, and this in a sport where so
often you need to build reputations
before you get anywhere near the
podium. They skate 30 hours a week.

Doris de Agostini
Ski downhill
Born: April 28, 1958, Airolo,
   Switzerland
Height: 5–10.   *Weight:* 132.
Career Highlights
Olympic Games: *downhill:* 17th, 1980;
   18th, 1976.
World Championships: *downhill:*

bronze medal, 1978; seventh, 1982.
World Cup: *overall:* tenth, 1983; 13th,
1981; 16th, 1982; 21st, 1980; 24th,
1976; 28th, 1977; *downhill:* first,
1983; second, 1981, 1982.

A girl of many talents – she likes knitting, cycling, volleyball and walking as
well as winning ski races, which she's
been doing for a long time. Her rise to
the top was hampered in 1980 by
injury, but now, having won the World
Cup downhill title in 1983, all that is a
distant memory for a woman who
enchants by her looks as well as her
speed.

She started quietly in 1983 with a
15th at Sansicario, then struck at
Montfano. Going 12th on the start list,
she was down in 1 min. 24.57 secs., and
the only moment of real danger came
from the next racer, France's Elisabeth
Chaud, who had a time of 1:24.69.
Doris was sixth at Megeve, second in
another race there and won at Les
Diablerets. Then she was tenth at
Jahorina and fifth at Mont Tremblant
to clinch the title.

Christopher Dean
Ice dancer
Born: July 27, 1958, Nottingham,
England.
Height: 5–10.   *Weight:* 154.
Career Highlights
Olympic Games: fifth 1980.
World Championships: gold medal
1981, 1982, 1983; fourth 1980; eighth
1979; 11th 1978.
European Championships: gold medal
1981, 1982; fourth 1980; sixth 1979;
ninth 1978.
British Championships: gold medal
1978, 1979, 1980, 1981, 1982; bronze
1977; fourth 1976.

See **Jayne Torvill**

Paolo de Chiesa
Ski slalom
Born: March 14, 1956, Saluzzo, Italy.
Height: 5–9. *Weight:* 175.
Career Highlights
World Championships: *slalom:* fourth, 1982.
World Cup: *overall:* tenth, 1975; 16th, 1982; 23rd, 1978; 27th, 1983; *slalom:* eighth, 1983.

The great Italian tradition in slalom ski racing – at Innsbruck in the Winter Olympic Games in 1976, Piero Gros won the gold medal and Gustavo Thoni the silver – is being maintained, although on a less exalted level, by de Chiesa who concentrates on the slalom itself, not the giant slalom. He has had a long, hard road to the top and although he is only 27 he can look a lot older. 1983 was a good season: seventh at Courmayeur, fifth at Madonna, fourth at Parpan, fifth at Kitzbuehel, fourth at Kranjska Gora, second behind Ingemar Stenmark at Markstein, eighth at Tarnaby and sixth at Gallivare.

Laurent Depouilly
Singles figure skater
Born: October 26, 1963, Asnieres, France.
Height: 5–5. *Weight:* 133.
Career Highlights
World Championships: 11th 1983.
European Championships: ninth 1983.
French Championships: silver medal 1983; fifth 1982.

Laurent Depouilly made his big debut in the 1983 European Championships and surprised many people by finishing as high as ninth. The 19-year-old had only been skating since 1973 and because France's leading men's skater, Jean-Christophe Simond, has hinted that he'll retire after the 1984 Winter Olympics, Depouilly looks set to become undisputed French number one.

In the World Championships he was 11th – 12th in the figures, 13th in the short programme and 11th in the free skating. A student, his hobbies are cycling, tennis, volley-ball, cinema and music. He is coached by Robert Dureville.

Ariane Ehrat
Ski downhill
Born: February 17, 1961, Schaffhausen, Switzerland.
Height: 5–4. *Weight:* 125.
Career Highlights
World Championships: *downhill:* 14th, 1982.
World Cup: *overall:* 37th, 1983; *downhill,* tenth, 1983.

The girl who likes tennis, windsurfing, jazz ballet, reading and cooking is one of the rising names in women's ski racing. From finishing only sixth in the Swiss Championships downhill in 1980, she had a good debut in the 1982 World Cup with a fifth place at Saalbach, and then 14th in the downhill at the World Championships in Schladming. Her progress continued in 1983 with an eighth at Sansicario, a seventh at Megeve, a third at Jahorina.

Claudine Emonet
Ski downhill
Born: February 13, 1962, Sallanches, France.
Height: 5–3. *Weight:* 110.
Career Highlights
World Cup: *overall:* 30th, 1983; *downhill:* eighth, 1983; 19th, 1982.

French ski racing is getting back onto its feet, thanks to several youngsters.

Claudine is one who is advancing rapidly. She almost created a great surprise in the first downhill of the 1983 season, at Sansicario, when, starting 28th she was only 29 hundredths of a second behind the winner, Caroline Attia – another French girl. She couldn't maintain anything like that for the next two races, but was fifth at Megeve and eighth at Jahorina. She finished the season with an 11th place at Mont Tremblant, Canada.

Karin Enke
Speed skater
Born: June 20, 1961, Dresden, East Germany.
Height: 5–7.   *Weight:* 158.
Career Highlights
Olympic Games: *500 metres:* gold medal, 1980.
World Championships: *combined:* gold medal, 1982; *sprints:* gold medal, 1980, 1981.

Karin Enke.

29

Karin's mother wanted her brother, Holger, to skate and took him along to the rink in Dresden. Karin, then only four, had to go, too, but she found watching her brother train extremely boring. A coach, Anne-Marie Halbach, noticed Karin and managed to find a pair of skates small enough.

By 1977, she had become good enough to produce a superb free skating programme in the East German championships and go on to Helsinki for the European Figure Skating Championships, where she was ninth overall. But she realised she could not get much further in figure skating so decided on the spot to change to speed skating. After a mere 14 days training she had managed a world class time of 2 mins. 30 secs. for the 1500 metres. And 18 months later, working towards the 1980 Winter Olympic Games, she became world sprint champion in Madison, Wisconsin. A week later at Lake Placid, she struck gold in the 500 metres, beating Leah Mueller (United States) and Natalia Petrusjeva (U.S.S.R.). Unfortunately for the ladies, Lake Placid was where the American Eric Heiden won a staggering five gold medals – at 500m, 1,000m, 1,500m, 5,000 and 10,000m.

Hans Enn.

Hans Enn

Ski giant slalom

Born: May 10, 1958, Saalfelden, Austria.
Height: 5–5.   *Weight:* 141.
Career Highlights
Olympic Games: *giant slalom:* bronze medal, 1980; *slalom:* fourth, 1980.
World Championships: *giant slalom:* sixth, 1978, 1982; *slalom:* 11th, 1978.
World Cup: *overall:* seventh, 1980; 12th, 1979; 13th, 1982; 14th, 1981; 20th, 1983; *giant slalom:* second, 1980; fourth, 1982; fifth, 1983.

They call Enn *sympathique,* which means a nice sort of bloke. For a while now he's concentrated on the giant slalom and his best result – the bronze medal at Lake Placid – came in this discipline. That year he finished second in the World Cup giant slalom table, too. 1983 wasn't quite so happy for him. Form guide: sixth at Val d'Isere, a good second place at Madonna, 12th at Adelboden, then victory at Kranjska Gora from Max Julen and Ingemar Stenmark, third at Garmisch, ninth at Aspen, fifth at Vail and fourth at Furano.

Irene Epple

Ski racer

Born: June 18, 1957, Seeg, West Germany.
Height: 5–3.   *Weight:* 119.
Career Highlights
Olympic Games: *giant slalom:* silver

Irene Epple.

medal, 1980; 15th, 1976; *downhill:* tenth, 1976; 19th, 1980.

World Championships: *giant slalom:* fourth, 1978; 14th, 1982, *downhill:* silver medal, 1978; eighth, 1982; 34th, 1974.

World Cup: *overall:* second, 1982; third, 1979; fifth, 1980, 1981; sixth 1983; tenth, 1976; 11th, 1978; 13th, 1975; 18th, 1977; *giant slalom:* first, 1982; seventh, 1983.

The girl who found fame as Sebastian Coe's girlfriend has been at the top of her sport for a generation and more. The last phase of her career has been distinctly interesting. Season 1980 began badly when she fell at Val d'Isere, but she recovered magnificently and in the Olympic Games in Lake Placid took the silver medal in the giant slalom, beaten only by arch-rival Hanny Wenzel.

The next World Cup season she won the giant slalom at Val d'Isere but otherwise had a poor result in the slaloms. To balance that, her downhill was strong, with a second and two third places. She maintained the downhill form in 1982 and was good enough in the giant slalom to win that overall first title. The record is worth setting down: first at Val d'Isere, third at Pila, second at Chamonix, first at Pfronten, fourth at Oberstaufen, third at Aspen, first at Waterville Valley, ninth at Alpe d'Huez, sixth at Sansicario. In terms of flair and consistency, this is ski racing of the highest quality.

1983 had its disappointments, although she did win a giant slalom at Verbier, then slotted in to her consistency again: third in another race the next day at Verbier, fifth at Megeve, eighth at Waterville Valley, then tenth in another race there. In the downhill, she was sixth at Schruns and 12th at Megeve.

Maria Epple
Ski racer

Born: March 11th, 1959, Seeg, West Germany.

Height: 5–5.   *Weight:* 121.

Career Highlights

Olympic Games: *giant slalom:* eighth, 1980; 24th 1976.

World Championships: *giant slalom:* gold medal, 1978; 23rd, 1982; *slalom:* sixth, 1982.

World Cup: *overall:* fourth, 1982; seventh, 1978; ninth, 1983; 14th, 1981; *giant slalom:* third, 1983; *slalom:* 11th, 1983.

The younger sister of the famous Irene, she suffered – and recovered from – a serious injury at the beginning of the 1978-79 World Cup and lost the whole of that season. She was already an outstanding giant slalom expert, having won the 1978 World Championships at Garmisch. In 1982 she won races at Oberstaufen, Aspen and Sansicario. She has never quite matched the all-round excellence of her sister, but her 1983 formguide in the giant slalom is good with seconds at Mont Tremblant and Waterville Valley.

Alexander Fadeev
Singles figure skater

Born: January 4, 1964, Kazan, U.S.S.R.

Height: 5–4.   *Weight:* 130.

Career Highlights

World Championships: fourth 1983; tenth 1982.

European Championships: bronze medal 1983; fifth 1982.

U.S.S.R. Championships: gold medal 1983.

Skate Moscow: winner 1982.

Fadeev was born – and spent his childhood – in Kazan, capital of the

Maria Epple.

Alexander Fadeev.

Tartar Autonomous Republic, and is now the leading Soviet men's skater. Officially the Soviets say: *'Fadeev flawlessly performs three-and-a-half revolution jumps and has now included another unique element – a combination of two triple jumps (Lutz and toe loop) in his new programme. Fadeev is one of those skaters who want to stun the world. If someone else makes a four-turn jump on ice (the much publicised quadruple jump), he will find something even more spectacular.'*

If Fadeev hasn't yet stunned the world, he's moving in the right direction. He was third at the U.S.S.R. championships in 1982 (behind Bobrin and Kotin), but impressed John Curry at the 1982 European Championships – in the short programme he landed a double flip-triple toe loop, and in the long a triple Lutz, loop, Salchow and three toe loops. He was tenth in the 1982 World Championships, behind Igor Bobrin (seventh, now retired), but above Vladimir Kotin (11th). His improvement was marked by a surge to third place in the 1983 European Championships – ninth in the compulsory figures, but third in the short programme, second in the free. And in the World Championships in Helsinki, he was sixth in the figures, fourth in the short, fourth in the free. The man who likes books and music is clearly a name to watch.

William Fauver
Pairs skater
Born: March 2, 1954, Shaker Heights, Ohio, U.S.A.
Height: 5–9. *Weight:* 150.
Career Highlights
World Championships: seventh 1983; eighth 1982.
United States Championships: silver medal 1981, 1983; bronze 1982.
Skate America: second 1982.
N.H.K. Trophy: fourth 1982.

See **Lea Ann Miller.**

Graeme Ferguson
Biathlete
Born: June 17, 1952. Fife, Scotland.
Height: 5–8. *Weight:* 175.
Career Highlights
Olympic Games: *20 kilometres:* 30th, 1976.
World Cup: *20 kilometres:* 36th, 1983.

Fergy, as he is known, has been a sub-aqua diver and a cyclist; he climbs, he canoes – and he has played for Raith Rovers. He has also captained the British biathlon team. A military man, like most biathletes, he has served with the Fourth Armoured Division Engineer Regiment in West Germany.
Ferguson was 30th (of 51) at the 1976 Olympics at Innsbruck in the 20 kilometres – a good result for a British biathlete, considering the ferocity of competition.

Heiko Fischer
Singles figure skater
Born: February 25, 1960, Stuttgart, West Germany.
Height: 6–2. *Weight:* 162.
Career Highlights
World Championships: eighth 1983.
European Championships: fourth 1983; sixth 1982.
West German Championships: gold medal 1982, 1983; bronze 1980, 1981.

Who is the best skater in West Germany? It's a question many have pondered since Norbert Schramm won their national championship in 1981. Fischer, a student of physics, took it from him in 1982. In 1981, he'd won events at St. Gervais and Obertsdorf and then, at Mannheim in January 1982, he brushed aside Schramm and Rudi Cerne with nine triples in his free programme.
It is to be expected, of course, for the national champion to do better in international competition than the man he has beaten, never mind the one who came third – in this case Schramm. But in the 1982 Europeans, Schramm took the gold medal, with Cerne fourth and Fischer back in sixth place. In 1983 Fischer was again German champion. He and Schramm went off to the European championships in Dortmund. Schramm retained his title with Fischer fourth, and it continued through to the World Championships in Helsinki, where Schramm won the silver with Fischer eighth.
Many Germans think that Fischer's performance is affected by nerves, although the man himself disagrees. He lists his hobbies as tennis, cycling, reading and music.

Paul Frommelt
Ski slalom
Born: August 9, 1957, Schaan, Liechtenstein.
Height: 5–7. *Weight:* 144.
Career Highlights
World Championships: *slalom:* bronze medal, 1978.
World Cup: *overall:* tenth, 1977; 17th, 1979, 1981; 25th, 1980; *slalom:* third, 1977; eighth, 1982; 14th, 1983.

Older brother Willi got a bronze medal in the slalom at the 1976 Winter Olympic Games and a bronze medal in the 1974 World Championships at St. Moritz in the downhill. Paul Frommelt showed his promise in 1977, finishing second behind Ingemar Stenmark twice in World Cup races. (He was ill with gastric problems for the second of those, at Wengen, and decided to ski at the last moment). In his second run he was a mere 0.98 behind Stenmark. His first victory came in 1979 at Crans Montana in a slalom.

Season 1980-81 was a fine one: second at Madonna di Campiglio, behind Stenmark of course, third at Garmisch, ninth at Wengen, seventh at Oslo, eighth at Are. The next season was not nearly so good – fourth at Madonna, third at Wengen, eighth at Bad Wiessee and seventh at Kitzbuehel. 1983 was not good either. He abandoned at Madonna, abandoned at Kitzbuehel, was fifth at Kranjska Gora, ninth at Markstein, sixth at St. Anton, 19th at Markstein again, tenth at Tarnaby, missed a gate at Gallivare and did not finish the second run at Furano, Japan.

Jana Gantnerova-Soltysova
Ski downhill
Born: September 30th, 1958, Kezmarok, Czechoslovakia.
Height: 5–5. *Weight:* 134.
Career Highlights
Olympic Games: *giant slalom:* 21st, 1980; 25th, 1976; *downhill:* tenth, 1980; 33rd, 1976.
World Championships: *downhill:* 19th, 1978.
World Cup: *overall:* 13th, 1980; 21st, 1981; 29th, 1983; *downhill:* seventh, 1983; 28th, 1982.

The Czech girl's success in finishing seventh in 1983's World Cup downhill was all the more surprising because, after a long career, she had simply faded away in 1982. All that changed very quickly when she was sixth in the opening downhill in 1983 and seventh in the next one. Building on that she recorded a fifth and a sixth, before falling back to 33rd at Les Diablerets. Then a ninth and a 19th picked her up, results all the more praiseworthy considering her poor showing the season before had given her low start numbers.

Susan Garland
Pairs skater
Born: April 30, 1966, Bristol, England.
Height: 5–3. *Weight:* 105.
Career Highlights
World Championships: 13th, 1983.
European Championships: sixth 1982; eighth 1983.
British Championships: gold medal 1982.
St. Ivel: third 1982.
Ennia Challenge Cup: third 1982.

Until 1981, Susan skated with Robert Daw – finishing tenth in the 1980 Winter Olympics – and when that partnership ended she began skating with Ian Jenkins. Just a few months later in the European Championships at Lyons they were sixth, but then

Susan Garland and Ian Jenkins.

Susan sustained a bad injury which made them miss the World Championships.

Under trainer Anne Crompton, an unfailing optimist, they trained extremely hard during the summer at Solihull and won the British Championships, held there in December 1982. But the 1983 European Championships were a disappointment: Susan fell once and they could finish no higher than eighth, two places lower than in 1982. In the World Championships – their first – they were 13th (14th in the short programme, 13th in the free).

Susan, who also swims, dances and likes most sports, is a lively, almost irrepressible person, while Ian, nearly a foot taller and more than 50 pounds heavier, is quieter. Physically they seem the perfect blend and at moments can be superb – witness their cartwheel descent from a lift in the 1983 European Championships.

Joel Gaspoz
Ski slalom
Born: September 25, 1962, Morgins, Switzerland.
Height: 5–6. *Weight:* 149.
Career Highlights
Olympic Games: *giant slalom:* seventh, 1980.
World Championships: *giant slalom:* fourth, 1982; *slalom:* fifth, 1982.
World Cup: *overall:* seventh, 1982; 11th, 1981.

This lover of motorsport, music and tennis made an outstanding start to his career. His father is a former Swiss regional champion who runs a restaurant called La Bergerie (which was also the name of the hotel at Val d'Isere once run by a certain Killy family). In 1979, he was second in the slalom and third in the giant slalom at the European Junior Championships. In the 1979 Europa Cup he won the giant slalom at Tetovo and was second and third in two races at Courchevel. In 1981, also in the Europa Cup giant slalom, he won at Elm.

He looks very much a man of the times, with long, almost shaggy hair and a confident smile. That smile has been evident in his World Cup career, although in 1979 he was a victim of nerves and did not finish the courses at Steinach and Crans-Montana.

The nerves soon vanished. During the 1980 season he was second in the giant slalom at Saalbach (behind Ingemar Stenmark) and third at both Adelboden and Cortina d'Ampezzo. A new star was born. Everybody seemed amazed at his explosive breakthrough except Gaspoz himself. Not that he said as much. He is noted for his quietness and his modesty. He had spent time in England learning the language before that 1980 season and says: *'I like to travel, discover the world and foreign countries, but I am always happy to come home'.* Season 1981 was a time of consolidation: second at Morzine, third at Borovetz and fifth in a slalom at Kitzbuehel. Then 1982 and victory at Aprica, Italy, in the giant slalom. Phil Mahre was second and Stenmark third. The 1983 season was bitterly disappointing and he frequently vent his frustration by riding his 350cc motorbike very fast.

Bernhard Germeshausen
Bobsleigh
Born: August 21, 1951, Heiligemstadt, East Germany.
Height: 6–3. *Weight:* 211.
Career Highlights
Olympic Games: *two-man bob:* gold

The East German bobsleigh team.

medal, 1976; silver medal 1980; *four-man bob:* gold medal, 1976, 1980.

World Championships: *two-man bob:* silver medal, 1976, 1980; *four-man bob:* gold medal: 1976, 1977, 1980; silver medal, 1979; bronze medal, 1978.

European Championships: *two-man bob:* gold medal, 1979; silver medal, 1978, 1980, 1981, 1983; *four-man bob:* gold medal, 1979, 1981; silver medal, 1978.

The rarefied, dangerous and extremely fast world of bobsleigh racing is now openly dominated by two nations: East Germany and Switzerland. In the 1976 Winter Olympics, they took three of the first four places in the four-man and two of the first three places in the two-man competition. By 1980 and Lake Placid, their grip had become total: two-man: Erich Scharer and Josef Benz (Switz) 4:09.36, Germeshausen and Hans-J Gerhardt (E. Ger) 4:10.93, Meinhard Nehmer and Bogdan Musiol (E. Ger) 4:11.08. In the four-man: East Germany 3:59.92, then the Swiss, then the East Germans, including Horst Schoenau. In fact, the East Germans have an enormous advantage in that they possess an artificial track in the south of their country which has permanent ice from September; the Swiss, of course, have St. Moritz. Countries with tracks are East Germany, Austria, Romania, West Germany, Italy, Switzerland and the United States. But you cannot escape that two-way domination between East Germany and

Switzerland.

The 1982 World Championships at St. Moritz were another example. This time Scharer won the two-man with Max Ruegg, the East Germans taking the bronze. Just to show their strength, Schoenau was called in at the last moment to replace top drivers Lehman and Nehmer (both injured) and he was third in the two-man.

Because bobsleigh is a tight team sport, it's difficult to see the racers as anything more than protective helmets in a row and a sleek bob whistling by; but it does require enormous skill especially by the driver and brake-man. It also demands total fitness which the East Germans and the Swiss certainly have.

Marc Girardelli
Ski slalom
Born: July 18, 1963, Lustenau, Austria.
Height: 5–9.   *Weight:* 147.
Career Highlights
World Cup: *overall:* fourth 1983; sixth 1982; 26th 1981. *giant slalom:* third, 1982; sixth, 1983; 23rd, 1981; *slalom:* seventh, 1983; eighth, 1982; 15th, 1981.

Although he was born an Austrian, Girardelli made a decision in 1980 to race for Luxemburg after, it was reported, the Austrians had turned him down. All that changed in the World Cup event at Gallivare, Sweden, in 1983. Until then, Girardelli had established a reputation as someone who was always a runner up.

In the morning on the first run he got down the slalom course in 45.26 seconds. It had a vertical drop of 154 metres and 65 gates, and it was to claim many victims. Ingemar Stenmark was down in 45.75 secs. and another Swede, Stig Strand, in 45.76 secs.

Girardelli stormed it in the second run – 47.23 against Strand's 48.12 and Stenmark's 48.33. In the end it looked like this: Girardelli 1:32.49, Strand 1:33.88, Stenmark 1:34.08.

In 1983 he was runner-up again, however, with a second place in the giant slalom at Aspen. Other good results that season include: fourth at Kitzbuehel and at Tarnaby in the slalom and sixth at Todtnau in the giant slalom.

Laurie Graham
Ski downhill
Born: March 30, 1960, Inglewood, Ontario, Canada.
Height: 5–4.   *Weight:* 127.
Career Highlights
Olympic Games: *downhill:* 11th, 1980.
World Championships: *giant slalom:* 24th, 1982; *downhill:* bronze medal, 1982.
World Cup: *overall:* 18th, 1983; 23rd, 1980; *downhill:* fifth, 1983; 12th, 1982.

Laurie started ski-ing at four and racing at nine. In 1974 she was named in the Southern Ontario team and in 1977 in the national team for the Can-Am Finals. She listed her hobbies then as swimming, tennis, canoeing, music and reading. She is now, after a hard apprenticeship, one of the world's leading women downhillers. In 1980, she was showing her strength with three top ten places, one of them a third at Val d'Isere in the first race of the season. In 1982, she began with a fourth at Saalbach and was in the top ten three times more. 1983 went as follows: 11th at Sansicario, fourth at Schruns, 12th at Megeve, tenth at Les Diablerets, sixth at Jahorina, then a glorious and popular victory at Mont Tremblant, Canada.

Scott Gregory
Ice dancer
Born: July 31, 1959, Syracuse, New
  York, U.S.A.
Height: 5–8½.   *Weight:* 142.
Career Highlights
World Championships: seventh 1983;
  eighth 1982.
United States Championships: silver
  medal 1983; bronze medal 1982;
  fourth 1981.
Skate America: winner 1982.
Skate Canada: winner 1982.

See **Elisa Spitz**

Franz Gruber
Ski slalom
Born: November 8, 1959, Kirchdorf,
  Austria.
Height: 5–8.   *Weight:* 149.
Career Highlights
World Championships: *slalom:* eighth,
  1982.
World Cup: *overall:* 15th, 1982; 25th,
  1981.

The Austrian has made steady progress
since his debut in December 1978 at
Madonna di Campiglio where he had
the fourth fastest intermediate time on
the first run. He was already known in
Austria because he won their schools
championships (slalom and giant
slalom) and joined their national junior
team in 1974. By 1980 he had done his
national service and completed a
technical apprenticeship at ski
manufacturers, Fischer.
  He is a reliable ski racer and was six
times in the top ten in slalom during the
1981 World Cup season with a third
place at Are, Sweden. This impression
of reliability was reinforced in the next
season when he was in the top ten six
times, including a second place at Bad
Wiessee and a third at Kranjska Gora

to put him 15th in the World Cup
standings – his best performance by ten
places in his career, and only two
places behind the famous Hans Enn,
the leading Austrian slalomer.
  Gruber, who likes hunting and playing football – he was a member of the
Molln team in the Austrian League
Eastern Division – intends to join the
police when he retires.

Scott Hamilton
Singles figure skater
Born: August 28, 1958, Toledo, Ohio,
  U.S.A.
Height: 5–3.   *Weight:* 110.
Career Highlights
Olympic Games: fifth 1980.
World Championships: gold medal
  1981, 1982, 1983.
United States Championships: gold
  medal 1981, 1982, 1983.
Skate Canada: winner 1980.
Skate America: winner 1981, 1982.
N.H.K. Trophy: winner 1982.

Scott Hamilton's story is remarkable.
As a child he had an illness which stun-
ted his growth. He is only 5ft. 3in., but
now in full health – full enough to have
been world champion three times. He
was fifth in the 1980 Olympics and
again fifth in the World Championships
at Dortmund a few weeks later. Then a
whole new world opened up for him
when Jan Hoffman (East 'Germany),
Vladimir Kovalev (U.S.S.R.) and Britain's Robin Cousins retired. (Cousins,
of course, was trained by Carlo Fassi,
who at one time also trained Hamilton.
In fact Hamilton has had several
trainers: Evy Scotvold, Mary Scotvold,
Fassi, Pierre Brunet and now Donald
Laws).
  Hamilton – even with his triple Lutz
and triple Salchow jumps, which he
regards as his speciality – hasn't cap-

Scott Hamilton.

tured the imagination of the skating public in the way either John Curry or Cousins did. He likes water ski-ing, motor cycling and is addicted to American television soap operas.

In the 1983 World Championships in Helsinki, he was second in the compulsory figures behind France's Jean-Christophe Simond, then won the short programme (with two marks of 5.9) and the free skating where he did six triple-Lutz, two Salchows and three toe loops. He did stumble once. It was an extremely consistent performance and because Simond fell away, Hamilton became World Champion again easily from Norbert Schramm of West Germany. Scott incidentally became the first man to win three consecutive world titles since the Czech Nepela.

Franz Heinzer
Ski downhill
Born: April 11, 1962, Rickenbach, Switzerland.
Height: 5–9. *Weight:* 170.
Career Highlights
World Championships: *downhill:* fourth, 1982.
World Cup: *overall:* 26th, 1982, 1983; *downhill:* 19th, 1983.

This is one of the young lions of downhill racing, and one of a clutch of top Swiss. He started in 1981 with 43 points and a 36th place in the World Cup overall (a point better than Ken Read and six points better than Franz Klammer). He was third at Aspen and had three other top ten finishes. In the World Championships in Schladming in 1982, he was fourth. He arrived at that moment. And in mid-season, he came close to a real breakthrough – sixth at Crans Montana, tenth at Kitzbuehel, fourth at a second race at

Kitzbuehel, fifth at Wengen, ninth at Garmisch. He finished strongly too, with a sixth place at Aspen. But 1983 wasn't so happy, 14th at Pontresina, seventh and fourth in the two races at Val Gardena, then he missed the rest of the season with injury. His hobbies are motorcross, sport in general and music.

Nathalie Herve
Ice dancer
Born: March 28, 1963, Troyes, France.
Height: 5–3. *Weight:* 112.
Career Highlights
World Championships: 11th 1982.
European Championships: fifth 1983; sixth 1981, 1982.
St. Gervais: second 1981.
Morzine: second 1982.

Nathalie Herve and Pierre Bechu are comfortably the best French ice dance couple and have been there or thereabouts in international competitions for three years. They underlined this by finishing fifth in the 1983 European Championships at Dortmund (fifth in all sections). Unfortunately, they had to retire from the 1983 World Championships through illness after being ninth in the compulsory dances.

They train 32 hours a week in summer and 35 hours a week in winter. Both have varied interests: she enjoys cinema, dancing, photography and wind surfing; he likes cinema, classical music, tennis and wind surfing.

Erika Hess
Ski slalom
Born: March 6, 1962, Aeschi, Switzerland.
Height: 5–3. *Weight:* 116.
Career Highlights
Olympic Games: *slalom:* bronze medal, 1980.

Erika Hess.

World Championships: *giant slalom:*
gold medal 1982; ninth, 1978; *slalom:*
gold medal, 1982.
World Cup: *overall:* first, 1982; second,
1981; third, 1983; seventh, 1980;
15th, 1979; 28th, 1978; *giant slalom:*
fourth, 1983; *slalom:* first, 1983.

Erika Hess was raised on a small farm
and started to race when she was five,
leaving school at 15 to compete full
time. But even when she started to do
well, people called her 'timid'. The star
quality was yet to come. By 1980, with
a bronze medal at the Lake Placid
Olympics in the slalom safely gathered
in, she was saying: *'With a little bit of
luck, I would have really been able to
arrive, but I am not consumed by
impatience. I'm only 18.'* At the age of
15, she had taken second place behind
the great Lise-Marie Morerod in the
Swiss Championships giant slalom in
1977. She also tried her hand at

downhills but confessed. *'I am a little
bit frightened by the speed.'*

The great year – 1982 – was not far
away for the girl who likes watersports
and knitting. She went to the World
Championships at Schladming and won
the slalom from the American Christin
Cooper and the giant slalom again from
Cooper. In the World Cup slaloms she
was irresistible finishing 2,1,1,1,1,3,1,
and in the giant slalom 2,4,3,2,3,2,4,1,2
– enough to give her a winning 297
points. Irene Epple (West Germany)
was next with 282.

Any hopes of retaining the World
Cup title were battered in 1983 by the
emergence of American Tamara
McKinney, although Erika went the
distance. In theory Hess still had a
chance of keeping her title in the last
two races in Japan. She needed to win
both and McKinney to finish far down.
But she was second to McKinney in the
slalom and tenth in the giant slalom.

Helmut Hoeflehner
Ski downhill
Born: November 24, 1959,
   Gumpenberg, Austria.
Height: 5–9.   *Weight:* 158.
Career Highlights
World Cup: *overall:* 24th, 1982, 1983;
downhill: tenth, 1983.

There is a production line of downhill
ski racers in Austria. Hoeflehner is one
of those who still has to prove himself
although the promise is there. He
began in 1980, 53rd overall in the
World Cup. In 1981, he was up to 30th,
and was on the move: fourth at Garmisch, sixth at Kitzbuehel and sixth at
Aspen. It was not maintained in 1982,
but 1983 ended with a victory at Lake
Louise, when Franz Klammer was
second and became World Cup
downhill champion. Hoeflehner's time:
1:40.52 against Klammer's 1:40.75.

Iavor Ivanov
Ice dancer
Born: April 22, 1964, Sofia, Bulgaria.
Height: 5–5.   *Weight:* 117.
Career Highlights
Bulgarian Championships: gold medal
   1981, 1982.

See **Hristina Boianova**

Susan-Ann Jackson
Figure skater
Born: November 30, 1965, Nottingham,
   England.
Height: 5–0.   *Weight:* 104.
Career Highlights
World Championships: fourth, B final,
   1983.
European Championships: fourth, B
   final, 1983.
British Championships: bronze medal,
   1982.

Skate Canada: sixth, 1982.
Skate America: ninth, 1982.

Susan is trained at Nottingham by
David Lunn, and is one of the most promising young British skaters. She
began 1982 by showing a lot of that
promise – ninth at Skate America and
sixth at Skate Canada. She was also
sixth at the St. Ivel.
   In 1983, she was chosen for the
British team at the European Championships at Dortmund, despite having
finished below Alison Southwood in the
British Championships. She was 23rd
in the compulsory figures, 20th in the
short programme and fourth in the 'B'
final. (The competition was controversially cut into two parts). In the World
Championship in Helsinki she was
fourth in the 'B' final and 19th overall.

Ian Jenkins
Pairs skater
Born: May 18, 1962, Bristol, England.
Height: 6–0.   *Weight:* 161.
Career Highlights
World Championships: 13th 1983.
European Championships: sixth 1982;
   eighth 1983.
British Championships: gold medal
   1982.
St. Ivel: third 1982.
Ennia Challenge Cup: third 1982.

See **Susan Garland.**

Kelly Johnson
Ice dancer
Born: September 27, 1961, Willowdale,
   Ontario, Canada.
Height: 5–2.   *Weight:* 105.
Career Highlights
World Championships: tenth 1983.
Canadian Championships: silver medal
   1983.

Skate Moscow: eighth 1982.
Zagreb Golden Spin: fourth 1982.

Both Kelly Johnson and John Thomas skated internationally with different partners (she with Kris Harber and he with Joanne French). Johnson and Thomas established their partnership in the spring of 1982 and in their first season were second, behind Tracy Wilson and Robert McCall, in the 1983 Canadian Championships at Montreal (third after the compulsory section, but second in the free dancing). In the free they skated to the music from *West Side Story* and, as one observer put it, *'they had so much feeling for the story behind the music.'* The Canadian Figure Skating Association feels they *'are both excellent dance technicians and skate with expression and power.'*

That result at Montreal earned them a place in the team for the 1983 World Championships at Helsinki, where they made a promising debut – 13th in the compulsory dance, 11th in the original set pattern, 10th in the free dance.

She likes dancing, reading and sewing; he prefers archery and pool.

Max Julen
Ski giant slalom
Born: March 15, 1961, Zermatt, Switzerland.
Height: 5–3. *Weight:* 141.
Career Highlights
World Championships: *giant slalom:* 13th, 1982.
World Cup: *overall:* eighth, 1983; *giant slalom:* second, 1983.

The young man who likes tennis and football launched his career in 1980 when, in the Europa Cup giant slalom, he was third at Zakopane and fifth at Tarvisio. He has made spectacular pro-gress since then and in 1983 was beaten by only seven points in the World Cup giant slalom – by world champion Phil Mahre. His 1983 results were: second at Adelboden, second at Kranjska Gora, 13th at Garmisch, second at Todtnau, second at Gallivare, fourth at Aspen, third at Vail, and second at Furano.

Alastair Kennedy-Rose
Bobsleigh
Born: September 5, 1959, Bournemouth, England.
Height: 6–2. *Weight:* 196.
Career Highlights
British Two-Man Championships: silver medal, 1982.
Nash & Dixon Trophy: Top British Brakeman, 1982/3.

Alastair Kennedy-Rose is a physical education student who arrived at bobsleighing via judo and the decathlon. When he graduates he plans to join the Royal Marine Commandos.

Bruno Kernen
Ski downhill
Born: March 25, 1961, Schonried, Switzerland.
Height: 5–5. *Weight:* 154.
Career Highlights
World Cup: *overall:* 22nd, 1983; *downhill:* 13th, 1983.

The young man whose profession is cooking began 1983 in the Swiss B team – in theory, anyway. He was picked for the first race in the senior team at Pontresina and finished 13th. At Val Gardena – where there were two races – he was 20th and tenth. And then, on the world-famous Hahnenkamm course at Kitzbuehel, came one of the season's great moments. Steve Podborski

(Canada) had the fastest time, 2 mins. 6.79 secs. But then, coming off start number 29, Kernen got down in 2:06.68, to win the race. The next day, in a second race on the same mountain, he was seventh; then 16th and seventh at Val d'Isere, 15th at Sarajevo, 12th at Aspen, tenth at Lake Louise. Switzerland already has a clutch of top downhillers. Here is another.

Franz Klammer
Ski downhill

Born: December 3, 1953, Mooswald, Austria.
Height: 6–1. *Weight:* 154.
Career Highlights
Olympic Games: *downhill:* gold medal, 1976.
World Championships: *downhill:* silver medal, 1974; fifth, 1978; seventh, 1982.
World Cup: *overall:* third, 1975, 1977; fourth, 1976; fifth, 1974, 1978; eighth, 1973; 14th, 1982; 18th, 1983; *downhill:* first, 1975, 1976, 1977, 1978, 1983; second, 1974; fifth, 1982.

Franz Klammer is the greatest downhill racer of all time. His name evokes powerful images of a man on a mountain taking awful risks, driving himself to the absolute limit – and winning. Helga Gold, in 1975 director of the Austrian Ski Federation, knew Klammer as a boy: *'From the beginning, when he was a raw 15-year-old, he used to fall, then get straight up and come back for more. We all saw immediately that he was made of tough timber.'*

Between 1974 and 1978 he won 22 races including, incredibly, six in a row to beat Jean-Claude Killy's record. In 1980, the Austrian Government estimated that tourists spent 110 million nights in Austria and spent 70 billion Austrian schillings (about £3.5 billion). Most come to ski and winning downhills is the best advertisement for that.

Klammer, from a hamlet in the south of Austria, is of farming stock. Even when he beat Killy's record, he described himself as a small-holder, *'chickens, potatoes, some cattle and a few goats.'* When he won the Olympic title at Innsbruck by .33 of a second in 1976 he went number 13, carrying the weight of the whole country. *'I was in the air so often I was sure I would fall,'* he said. He didn't and when he reached the finishing line he didn't have time to swivel and see if he'd won. Hundreds of people engulfed him.

He won the World Cup downhill titles in 1977 and 1978, but there was a moment at the Wold Championships in 1978 when people sensed the great days were drawing to a close. The rumour was that Klammer would be offered a million dollars to go professional in North America if he won. However, he couldn't find the magic and was fifth. There was a decline after that and he was not selected for the 1980 Olympic team (Charlie Kahr, who dropped him, had to have a police guard round his house, and protection for his family).

He lingered on but he was growing old for a downhiller: his body was not as supple as when he took the risks. *'I used to stand at the start and think: If I'm good today, I'll only be one and a half seconds behind the winner.'* For a downhiller, that sort of time is a chasm. *'I knew what people were thinking. It was in their eyes. "He's finished"'*

Then Kahr decided Klammer needed to change ski companies and at the same time Klammer started training like he had never trained before. The result was quite extraordinary. In the 1982/83 season he was second at Lagalp, third at Val Gardena, then –a second race at Val Gardena – he won, gloriously. So it came to Lake Louise in Canada for the World Cup downhill shoot out. Klammer had 86 points, but seven others could have caught him. He went 15th, got down the 2,903 metre course faster than the Swiss Conradin Cathomen –whom he had to beat – and the title was his. Klammer said: *'Never has it been so close among so many or the title won by so few points. It's a really great day.'*

Franz Klammer

Anna Kondrashova
Singles figure skater
Born: June 30, 1965, Moscow,
  U.S.S.R.
Height: 5–3. *Weight:* 106.
Career Highlights
World Championships: fifth 1983.
European Championships: fifth 1983.
U.S.S.R. Championships: silver medal
  1983.

Anna started skating in 1971, at the age
of six, because she caught colds so
often and her mother thought healthy
exercise might help. So she was taken
to a children's session at the Luzhniki
Central Stadium. A year later she
began to train at the popular Central
Army Figure Skating School and three
years ago she joined Eduard Pliner, the
famous coach. It wasn't easy for her to
get on with him at first: he's known to
be emotional and quick-tempered. But
she survived and after a year was
among the six best women skaters in
the U.S.S.R.

Up to the age of ten, she took music
lessons as well as skating and likes

Anna Kondrashova.

classical music, particularly Tchaikovsky's ballets. She lives in the Lenin Hills in Moscow and enjoys running in the nearby Moscow University park.

In the 1983 European Championships she was fifth, an extremely promising debut, and particularly caught the eye in the short programme and free skating. Moreover, she held fifth at the World Championships in Helsinki – ninth in the compulsory figures, fifth in the short and fifth in the free. She trains a programme which the Soviets claim to be the most complicated in world figure skating, including four different triple jumps and tricky choreography.

Vladimir Kotin
Singles figure skater
Born: March 28, 1962, Moscow, U.S.S.R.
Height: 5–8. *Weight:* 147.
Career Highlights
World Championships: ninth 1983; 11th 1982.
European Championships: fifth 1983; seventh 1982.
U.S.S.R. Championships: silver medal 1982; bronze medal 1983.
Skate Moscow: second 1982.

Kotin, coached by the famous Elena Tschaikowskaya, is very much the second Soviet Russian skater behind Alexander Fadeev. In the 1982 European Championships he was seventh, two places behind Fadeev; in the 1982 Worlds, he was up to 11th, one place behind Fadeev. In the 1983 Europeans he was up to fifth, but two places behind Fadeev. In his long programme he did seven triple jumps and his marks – around 5.5 were booed. In the 1983 Worlds he was ninth, Fadeev, of course, was fourth.

Bojan Krizaj
Ski slalom
Born: January 3, 1957, Kranj, Yugoslavia.
Height: 5–4. *Weight:* 149.
Career Highlights
Olympic Games: *giant slalom:* fourth, 1980; 18th, 1976.
World Championships: *slalom:* silver medal, 1982; 13th, 1974; *giant slalom:* seventh, 1982.
World Cup: *overall:* fourth, 1980; sixth, 1981; ninth, 1982, 1983; *slalom:* second, 1980; third, 1981; *giant slalom:* third, 1979.

Krizaj's father was a national Yugoslav ski champion. His son has done even better. Somebody described him four years ago as *'the bridgehead of a brilliant Yugoslavian team.'* The modest student of physical education would probably not comment on that, but the word brilliant lingers. He is now one of that rare group who competed in the 1974 World Championships and the 1976 Winter Olympics – 18th in the giant slalom, with a time of 3 mins. 35.90 secs. (1:49.08, 1:46.82), from the hopeless start position of 41.

His great dream was to become the first Yugoslav to win an Olympic medal in Alpine ski racing. It was not to be in Lake Placid – by two hundredths of a second. That was the margin he finished behind Austria's Hans Enn – 2 mins. 42.51 secs. against 2 mins. 42.53 secs. in the giant slalom. In the slalom, he missed a gate and that was that. But he did have one great moment that season, beating the immortal Ingemar Stenmark in a slalom at Wengen by 17 hundredths of a second.

He had a good season in 1981, with a second at Furano in the slalom, a third at Madonna di Campiglio and a third at Morzine in the giant slalom. And there was a sweet moment the

Bojan Krizaj.

next season – a victory in his native country over Stenmark, at Kranjska Gora, with 1 min. 38.89 secs. against 1 min. 38.93 secs.

That season he was to finish ninth, with one outstanding performance in the World Championships at Schladming in the slalom. Stenmark had the fastest time on the first run, and in the second the dangerous Mahre twins from America made mistakes. Stenmark didn't and neither did Krizaj, who got the silver medal (Stenmark 1 min. 48.48 secs. Krizaj 1 min. 48.90 secs.) In 1983 he started well in the slalom with a fifth at Courmayeur, a fourth at Madonna and a fifth at Gallivare. In the giant slalom he was ninth at Val d'Isere, and fourth at Adelboden.

Krizaj, a very good footballer, intends to become a professor of sports fitness.

Anni Kronbichler
Ski slalom
Born: March 22, 1963, Kufstein, Austria.
Height: 5–7.   *Weight:* 112.
Career Highlights
World Championships: *slalom:* 18th, 1982.
World Cup: *overall:* 11th, 1983; 22nd, 1982; *giant slalom:* 19th, 1983; *slalom:* sixth, 1983.

There was a moment of real promise when Anni began her World Cup career: she was ninth in a giant slalom at Limone Piemonte. Otherwise she was finding her way, with places in the late teens. The next season in the giant slalom the improvement was steady but not spectacular. In 1982 she was second twice, but victory remained elusive despite her optimistic smile until January, 1983. Then, starting

sixth at Schruns, she was a clear winner from Maria Rosa Quario (Italy) in the slalom. There was nothing comparable except for a very good fourth at Mont Tremblant, Canada, in the giant and a third at Maritor in the slalom.

Bernhard Lehmann
Bobsleigh
Born: November 11, 1948, Grossraeschern, East Germany.
Height: 6–1.   *Weight:* 207.
Career Highlights
Olympic Games: *four-man bob:* gold medal, 1976.
World Championships: *four-man bob:* gold medal, 1976; silver medal, 1982.
European Championships: *two-man bob:* gold medal, 1983; bronze medal, 1978; *four-man bob:* bronze medal, 1981.

See **Bernard Germeshausen**

Claudia Leistner
Singles figure skater
Born: April 15, 1965, Ludwigshafen, West Germany.
Height: 5–5.   *Weight:* 123.
Career Highlights
World Championshps: silver medal 1983; fourth 1982.
European Championships: bronze medal 1983; fifth 1982.
German Championships: silver medal 1982, 1983.
Skate America: second 1982.

The day after Claudia Leistner had won the silver medal in the 1983 World Women's Skating Championships in Helsinki, she still couldn't really believe it. She confessed as much in the foyer of the Inter-Continental Hotel, where a throng of people gathered round her to offer congratulations. At 17 she had

Claudia Leistner.

become both a celebrity and very much the up and coming skater in the world. And she hadn't even won her national championships – there she was beaten by Manuela Ruben.

Amazingly, until a couple of years ago Leistner was a highly competent roller skater who finished sixth in the 1982 world rollerskating championships. In figure skating she was fourth at her first attempt at a World Championship, at Copenhagen in 1982. The 1982-3 season was very much hers. At Skate America in October she was second, winning the short programme. And in the European Championships at Dortmund in February she won a bronze medal, despite being ninth in the compulsory figures. She attacked in the short programme with a super high double toe loop before her triple in her combination and was second. In the free she fell, but otherwise completed a full and excellent programme. At the Worlds, she actually improved on that – fifth in the figures, second in the short and third in the free for the silver medal.

She trains 25 hours a week in the summer, 35 in the winter and divides her time between America and West Germany. She is trained by Gunter Zoller and her hobbies include needlework, music, horse-riding and dancing.

Stanislav Leonovich
Pairs skater
Born: August 2, 1958, Sverdlovsk, U.S.S.R.
Height: 5–8. *Weight:* 158.
Career Highlights
Olympic Games: fourth 1980.
World Championships: silver medal 1982; sixth 1983.
European Championships: silver medal 1982.

U.S.S.R. Championships: gold medal 1983.

See **Marina Pestova**

Malcolm Lloyd
Bobsleigh
Born: February 26, 1947, Swansea, Wales.
Height: 5–10½. *Weight:* 201.
Career Highlights
Olympic Games: *four-man:* 13th, 1976; *two-man:* 20th, 1980.
British Four-man Championships: gold medal, 1981, 1982, 1983.
British Two-man Championships: gold medal, 1977, 1978, 1980, 1981, 1982, 1983.

Back in 1964, Tony Nash and Robin Dixon won an Olympic gold medal for Britain in the two-man bob at Innsbruck. Since then a great deal has changed: competition is harder, the resources needed are greater. Perhaps the increase in sophistication is best illustrated by the bobbers. For a decade and a half, the Britons have been outnumbered and outgunned, although remaining a cheerful, slightly irreverent lot.

Lloyd, who began in 1970, and won both the two-man and four-man titles in the 1983 Peter Stuyvesant British Championships at Igls, Austria, lists under hobbies: *No time, too busy looking after Hammond* (team manager). The man who shared his two-man triumph, Peter Brugnani, lists his as collecting hotel ashtrays and watching bootleg videos. David McMorrow settled for studies of late Twentieth Century European public house decor.

All this cannot disguise the fact that bobbing is dangerous. Unladen, a two-man bob weighs about 400lbs and a four-man about 950. And they travel at

British bobsleigh team.

90 miles an hour.

Because of the cost and difficulties of training, the British have tended to draw the majority of their bobbers from the armed services. Although they are working hard, there is a long way to go. At the .1983 World Championships at Lake Placid, Lloyd's four-man team was only tenth (Brugnani was in the bob with him). Although the star roles of driver and brakeman are to some extent interchangeable between two-man and four-man teams, names to watch for are Lloyd himself (a survivor of at least 23 crashes), Brugnani, and Nick Phipps.

Birgit Lorenz
Pairs skater
Born: August 2, 1963, Berlin, East Germany.
Height: 4–11.   *Weight:* 88.
Career Highlights
World Championships: seventh 1982; eighth 1983.

European Championships: bronze medal 1983; seventh 1982.
East German Championships: silver medal 1982.

In many ways Birgit Lorenz and her pairs skating partner Knut Schubert (coached by the lady with the most exotic name .in skating, Heide-Marie Walther-Steiner) were one of the big disappointments of the 1983 World Championships.

Earlier in the 1983 European Championships they had taken the bronze medal and during their performance a French judge marked them above defending champions Sabine Baess and Tassilo Thierbach. In fact, had Birgit not made a mistake on the change foot camels, they might have been up in first place after the short programme. During the warm up for the free programme she fell and struck the barrier and fell again on the throw triple Salchow during the programme, so that they were only third in that section and third overall. Despite falling, Birgit said she was extremely happy to get a medal.

What the pair couldn't do was sustain this in the 1983 World Championships at Copenhagen, when they were seventh in both the short and free, finishing eighth overall.

Peter Luescher
Ski slalom and downhill
Born: October 14, 1956, Romanshorn, Switzerland.
Height: 5–7.   *Weight:* 159.

Career Highlights
Olympic Games: *slalom:* eighth, 1976.
World Championships: *overall:* silver medal, 1982; *giant slalom:* seventh, 1978.
World Cup: *overall:* first, 1979; fifth, 1983; ninth, 1980; *downhill:* fifth, 1983; *giant slalom:* second, 1979; seventh, 1983; *slalom:* sixth, 1979.
Europa Cup: *overall:* second, 1981; *giant slalom:* second, 1981; *slalom:* third, 1981.
Swiss Championships: *overall:* gold medal, 1976; *giant slalom:* gold medal, 1979; *slalom:* gold 1980.

Peter Luescher

The man who likes tennis, motorsport, waterski-ing and travel is one of the most experienced ski racers in the world, and, unusually, good at both downhill and the giant slalom in a sport where specialisation is often deemed to be everything. In fact, in 1977, Luescher was competing in the slalom as well. Even in those days he talked lucidly about what he was doing – and why.

In 1979, he became overall World Cup winner, second in the giant slalom behind Ingemar Stenmark, sixth in the slalom. (The downhill assaults were yet to come in earnest, although he was 16th at Garmisch and 18th at Kitzbuehel). The title was achieved with astonishing consistency: in the slalom, 2,17,8,17,1,7,15,14, in the giant slalom, 2,2,2,2,9,3,5,7. He said when he'd won: *'You can't imagine before you hold it the weight of the crystal globe symbolising the World Cup. You think it's a piece of glass about the same size as any other, but when you've got it in your hands you quickly change your mind. After a few minutes it weighs a ton.'*

He remembered 'with emotion' the 1976 Olympic Games at Innsbruck when he finished eighth, and was determined to get a medal four years later at Lake Placid. It was not to be. He fell in both the slalom and giant slalom. There was consolation in 1982 when he took the silver medal at the World Championships in the combined.

In 1983 in the downhills, he was 26th at Pontresina and that set the tone for the early part of the season; then a splendid seventh at Kitzbuehel one day, eighth in another race the next. He was second at Val d'Isere, sixth at Sarajevo and won at St. Anton from another Swiss, Silvano Meli. In the giant slalom, he was second at Val d'Isere and won at Garmisch by 20 hundredths of a second.

Jacques Luthy
Ski slalom
Born: July 11, 1959, Charmey, Switzerland.
Height: 5–7.   *Weight:* 159.
Career Highlights
Olympic Games: *giant slalom:* fifth, 1980; *slalom:* bronze medal, 1980.
World Cup: *overall:* sixth, 1980; 13th, 1979; 15th, 1981; 17th 1983; 19th, 1982; *giant slalom:* third, 1980; fifth, 1979; 13th, 1982; tenth, 1983; *slalom:* 14th, 1982; 13th, 1983.
Swiss Championships: *overall:* gold medal, 1979, 1980.

Luthy announced himself immediately on the World Cup circuit. In the giant slalom in the 1979 season he was third at Adelboden and Are, and fifth overall. The next season he had a second place and two thirds, one of them in a slalom at Kitzbuehel.

The Lake Placid Olympics of 1980, were also a success for him. His time of 1 min. 45.06 secs. in the slalom got the bronze medal and he was beaten only by the two best slalom racers of modern times, Ingemar Stenmark and Phil Mahre. He was fifth in the giant slalom. But he could not really break through in the next season, with his best result a fourth at Adelboden; nor had he any more success in 1982.

His 1983 form: in the slalom 14th at Courmayeur, 14th at Madonna, then – suddenly – a second place (behind Phil Mahre's brother, Steve), sixth at Markstein, 14th at St. Anton, eighth in the second race at Markstein, 19th at Gallivare. Giant slalom: 16th at Val d'Isere, 22nd at Madonna, third at Adelboden, seventh at Kranjska Gora, seventh at Garmisch, sixth at Gallivare, 15th at Aspen.

He enjoys football and windsurfing when he can spare the time from practising on the slopes.

Jacques Luthy.

Phil Mahre

Phil Mahre
Ski slalom
Born: May 10, 1957, White Pass,
Washington, U.S.A.
Height: 5–9. *Weight:* 180.
Career Highlights
Olympic Games: *giant slalom:* fifth,
1976; tenth, 1980; *slalom:* silver
medal, 1980; *downhill:* 14th, 1980.
World Cup: *overall:* first, 1981, 1982,
1983; second, 1978; third, 1979,
1980; ninth, 1977; 14th, 1976; *giant
slalom:* first, 1982, 1983; third, 1978,
1981; fourth, 1977; fifth, 1976;
slalom: first, 1982; second, 1979,
1981; third, 1978; sixth, 1983.

Phil Mahre was born at 5.48 a.m. on
May 10, 1957. His twin brother Steve
was born at 5.52. Their father was an
apple grower and the word is that he
was struggling then. We must suppose
the days of struggle have long gone:
(even a couple of years ago, the twins'
income was estimated at 100,000
dollars a year for 'expense' money from
sponsors). In those days, Phil used to
say: *'I'd probably be just as happy flat
broke. I think you participate in a sport
because it's fun, because you excel at it.'*

Whether ski racing – or at least
inhabiting the ever-moving ski circus –
remains fun now is another matter.
However, Phil Mahre, World Cup
overall champion for the past three
seasons – has given richly of his talent,
particularly in his epic duelling with the
other great master of slalom ski racing,
Ingemar Stenmark, not to mention
brother Steven. In 1981 in Bulgaria,
Phil could become World Cup slalom
champion being first or second
(Stenmark fell). However Steve beat
him, to the absolute amazement of all
there. *'If Steve had lost to me on pur-
pose, that would have made it a cheap
trophy for me.'* Three days later Phil
clinched the title by finishing second in

a thrilling giant slalom competition in
Switzerland.

Both brothers are home-spun,,
frank-talking people, and they move
together, like, as somebody said, *'one
person.'* Steve is an inch taller, but
when you see them together, don't bet
on which is which. That Phil is the better ski racer cannot be doubted. He is a
proficient downhiller and says he'd like
to win a downhill: *'it is the only major
challenge left for me.'* He finished ninth
at Aspen in 1983.

But the slaloms are his real world,
and that duel with Stenmark, which has
gone on for five great years. Amazingly,
in 1983, he had not won a race until
Aspen in March, but that one settled
the World Cup giant slalom title. *'If the
most consistent skier leads it doesn't
matter if he hasn't won a race,'* he said.
The date: Monday, March 7.
Stenmark, as ever, was on his heels and
had been winning races, always an
ominous sign. Mahre took the first run,
.13 of a second quicker than Stenmark,
and in another classic shoot out won
the second run as well.

In 1984 the twins are to race less.
The days of fun are gone. Steve says:
*'The negatives seem to have a way of
overpowering the positives. We both
believe that there is a lot more to life than
ski racing.'* Phil says: *This (1983) is the
worst year I've had. None of it means as
much to me as it has in the past. I've had
trouble holding my mind so that I can
concentrate on two runs in a row.'* In
fact, the twins took their families
around with them (Steve's wife Debbie
and daughter Ginger, Phil's wife Holly
and daughter Lindsay) but whether this
solved or created problems is a matter
of opinion. At least one man close to
the World Cup circuit has said that
because their families were there, the
twins were not together all the time, as
they used to be.

Phil and Steve Mahre.

Steve Mahre

Ski slalom
Born: October 5, 1957, White Pass,
Washington, U.S.A.
Height: 5–10.   *Weight:* 180.
Career Highlights
Olympic Games: *giant slalom:* 13th
1976, 15th 1980.
World Championships: *giant slalom:*
gold medal 1982; 16th 1978; *slalom:*
eighth 1978.
World Cup: *overall:* third 1982; fourth
1981; tenth 1979; 12th 1980, 1983.

Steve lives in the shadow of his identi-
cal twin brother, Phil, although he has
had his own moments. In fact, they
have had moments together: once at
Cortina in a special slalom, Steve won
from Phil by .08 of a second, the first
time brothers had ever done that. Their
mother, Mary, says: *'They were like one
person when they were growing up. Part
of the family, sure, but really more a part
of each other. They never bickered,
never.'* Certainly when they are ski racing, there is an amazing bond between
them. Steve's finest hour was a World
Championship giant slalom win in
1982.

Steve Mahre.

Michael Mair
Ski downhill
Born: February 13, 1962, Brunico, Italy.
Height: 6–1. *Weight:* 204.
Career Highlights
World Championships: *downhill:* tenth, 1982.
World Cup: *overall:* 21st, 1983; *downhill:* 14th, 1983; 21st, 1982.

The handsome Italian with a bush of dark hair and a broad, open smile is a man of the future. In 1982 his first season in the World Cup, he was tenth at Crans-Montana, and fifth at Garmisch. Bearing in mind that most racers need three or four full seasons before they reach their peak, it is a debut full of promise.

In 1983 he was 16th at Pontresina, 14th at Val Gardena, fifth at Val d'Isere, fourth at Sarajevo and encouragingly, second at Aspen.

Vladimir Makeev
Ski downhill
Born: September 11, 1957, Syava Kemerovo, U.S.S.R.
Height: 5–8. *Weight:* 169.
Career Highlights
Olympic Games: *downhill:* 22nd, 1980.
World Championships: *downhill:* sixth, 1982; ninth, 1978.
World Cup: *overall:* 14th, 1978; *downhill:* 20th, 1983.

Legend has it that Makeev, part of the Russian spearhead into World Cup ski racing, was told at ten that he was too old to think seriously of a racing career. Whoever told him was very wrong indeed. You can search the famous *Biorama Ski Magazine* for season 1977 for a mention of *any* Russian and not find one. That changed in 1978 when Makeev was ninth in the World Cham-

pionship downhill at Garmisch.

He has remained a highly competent member of the Russian team since then but has never quite exploded like team mate Valeri Tzyganov, although there were moments when he threatened to. In season 1982 he was 22nd in the overall downhill standings, nine points and two places behind Tzyganov. The big moment of that season came in the World Championships when he was sixth – one place in front of Franz Klammer. 1983 began badly, and by the end of it, he had only twice been in the top ten. The Soviet team has other members – Igor Judin, Aleksei Bogdanov, Sergeir Tchaadaev –but they are a long way behind Makeev.

Paul Martini
Pairs skater
Born: November 2, 1960, Woodbridge, Ontario, Canada.
Height: 5–11. *Weight:* 184.
Career Highlights
Olympic Games: ninth 1980.
World Championships: bronze medal 1983; fourth 1982; seventh 1981; 11th 1980.
World Junior Championships: gold medal 1978.
Canadian Junior Championships: gold medal 1978.
Canadian Championships: gold medal 1979, 1980, 1981, 1982, 1983.

See **Barbara Underhill.**

Robert McCall
Ice dancer
Born: September 14, 1958, Dartmouth, Nova Scotia, Canada.
Height: 5–5. *Weight:* 155.
Career Highlights
World Championships: sixth 1983;

Michael Mair.

tenth 1982.

Canadian Championships: gold medal 1982, 1983.

St. Ivel: fourth 1982.

Skate Canada: second 1982.

Ennia Challenge Cup: third 1981.

See **Tracy Wilson**

Tamara McKinney
Ski slalom

Born: October 16, 1962, Lexington, Kentucky, U.S.A.

Height: 5–4.   *Weight:* 115.

Career Highlights

World Championships: *giant slalom:* sixth, 1982.

World Cup: *overall:* first, 1983; sixth, 1981; ninth, 1982; 14th, 1980; *giant slalom:* first, 1981, 1983; fourth, 1982; *slalom:* second, 1983; 12th, 1982.

The fast lady from Kentucky became

Tamara McKinney.

the first American woman to win the World Cup overall title in 1983. She was born in blue grass country, the eighth and youngest child of a family noted for ski-ing and riding horses. (Her mother was a ski instructor. Her half-brother Steve broke the 200 kilometres an hour barrier in speed ski-ing. Her sister Sheila was badly injured in a downhill in 1977).

She joined the 'white circus' when she was only 15. *'I was very distracted by everything. I was looking around in every direction. It was so new and so confusing. Now I've calmed down.'* Nicholas Howe, an American writer, captured her exactly: *'Tamara's touch on snow is phenomenal. She has this skittering, cascading laugh, and it is a perfect metaphor for the way she skis. Tamara just plain loves speed.'* Tamara finished third in her first big race in Europe – at 15. That was a slalom at Piancavallo, when she started way back on the start list. Perhaps it was an omen. She climbed steadily, although in 1982 she was troubled by a fractured right hand.

But in 1983 – a season which had a slow start for everybody because of conditions in the Alps – she peppered in the results: a victory in a slalom at Limone Piemonte, another at Davos; third and fourth in giant slaloms at Verbier, then a victory at Megeve, where she was nearly a second faster than another American Christin Cooper. By the time the racers had reached North America at the end of the season (only Japan remained) she had virtually clinched the World Cup. At the end of a tremendous week she had won two giant slaloms at Waterville Valley, New Hampshire and one at Vail. Erika Hess (Switzerland) needed to win at Furano, Japan, to rob McKinney. But McKinney won the giant slalom with Hess second.

Brad McStravick
Bobsleigh
Born: May 25, 1956, Sheffield, England.
Height: 6–0.   *Weight:* 182.
Career Highlights
Olympic Games: 15th in decathlon, 1980.

He's one of three decathletes drawn to bobbing. (Nick Phipps and Alastair Kennedy-Rose   are   the   others). McStravick, a part-time teacher, was actually 15th in the decathlon in the Moscow Olympics. He started bobbing only in late 1982. His hobbies are wine making, tennis and sub aqua.

Silvano Meli
Ski downhill
Born: August 11, 1960, Leysin, Switzerland.
Height: 5–6.   *Weight:* 162.
Career Highlights
World Cup: overall: 19th, 1983; 21st, 1982; *downhill:* 12th, 1983; 15th, 1982.
Swiss Championships: *downhill:* gold medal, 1978.

Meli is one of a very strong Swiss ski team. In his first season as a downhiller in the 1981 World Cup he was fifth at Aspen, Colorado. In 1982 he was ninth at Val d'Isere and tenth at Val Gardena. He had a total of 42 points which put him ahead of a lot more experienced racers.

In 1983 he was 11th at Pontresina, 57th and 18th at Val Gardena, eighth and fourth at Kitzbuehel, seventh and ninth at Val d'Isere, tenth at Sarajevo, second at St. Anton behind Peter Luescher, 16th at Aspen and 12th at Lake Louise.

He   enjoys   playing   tennis   for relaxation.

Isabella Micheli
Ice dancer
Born: March 30, 1962, Milan, Italy.
Height: 5–3. *Weight:* 110.
Career Highlights
World Championships: 11th 1983.
European Championships: eighth
  1983; 13th 1982.
Italian Championships: gold medal
  1982.

Isabella and her partner Roberto Pelizzola made a big impression in the 1983 European Championships at Dortmund, finishing eighth (in fact eighth in all sections), despite the fact that they only began to skate together in 1982. Before that, Pelizzola skated with Elisabetta Parisi and they were 11th in the 1981 European Championships.

They are trained by Joan Slater and Paola Mezzadri. They had a good World Championships in 1983 in Helsinki (12th in the compulsory dances, 10th in the original set pattern, 11th in the free programme). She likes music, dancing and reading; he enjoys music and electronics.

Lea Ann Miller
Pairs skater
Born: January 22, 1961, San Rafael,
  California, U.S.A.
Height: 5–3. *Weight:* 105.
Career Highlights
World Championships: seventh 1983;
  eighth 1982.
United States Championships: silver
  medal 1981, 1983; bronze 1982.
Skate America: second 1982.
N.H.K. Trophy: fourth 1982.

With her partner William Fauver, Lea Ann Miller is now ranked second in American pairs skating after the Carruthers, who easily beat them in the 1983 United States Championships. In fact, Miller and Fauver were third in the short programme (behind the Carruthers, and Jill Watson and Burt Lancon), but took the silver medal in the free skating with a performance which included good flying camel spins and a back inside death spiral. Alas, Miller had a two footed landing at one point – the only blemish.

At the 1983 World Championships they were eighth in the short programme and sixth in the free for an overall seventh place.

They are both college students and have made steady progress since 1979, when they were fifth in the United States Championships.

Mark Moore
Cross country ski
Born: September 28, 1961, Farnham
  Common, Buckinghamshire,
  England.
Height: 5–9. *Weight:* 156.
Career Highlights
Dobbiaco: *15 kilometres:* 25th, 1983.

Britain's cross country team, which is dominated by the Services and has 11 members, was formed only on February 1, 1983. They face incredible opposition: at the 1980 Olympics, the 15 medals in mens' events went to Sweden, Norway, Finland, the U.S.S.R., East Germany and Bulgaria.

Mark Moore is notable because the sport runs in his family. His father John was British Champion five times, biting away all his front teeth as he forced himself over the undulating, exhausting courses.

The Olympics are contested at 15, 30 and 50 kilometres with a four x ten kilometre relay for men. The women's distances are five and ten kilometres with a four x five kilometre relay.

Peter Mueller
Ski downhill
Born: October 6, 1957, Lambach, Switzerland.
Height: 5–9. *Weight:* 173.
Career Highlights
Olympic Games: *downhill:* fourth, 1980.

World Championships: *downhill:* fifth, 1978, 1982.
World Cup: *overall:* fourth, 1982; fifth, 1981; fifth, 1983; *downhill:* first, 1979, 1980; equal first, 1982; third, 1981; seventh, 1983.
Swiss Championships: *giant slalom:* gold medal, 1977; *downhill:* gold medal, 1979, 1980.

Peter Mueller.

Sport runs in Mueller's family – his parents were Swiss badminton doubles champions. He was spurred into becoming a champion skier when he moved, as a boy, to the Swiss mountain village of Adliswil – *'when one comes to the village, one is of necessity a less good skier than the mountain people who have grown up, skis on their feet, and have practised the sport for months, several hours a day. How many times have I heard them say to each other: Look at that Mueller – he comes to the village and he doesn't know how to ski.'* Mueller determined to show them.

At 18, in 1975, he was racing in the Europa Cup. By 1977, he was ready for an extraordinary assault on the world's downhill courses. His ability to glide earned him the nickname 'Superglider'. He is also known as a perfectionist. In the World Championships in Garmisch in 1978, there were signs of what was to come when he finished fifth. In 1979, he was supreme over the season, but in 1980 the Olympics eluded him – he was fourth. No matter. Over the 1980 season he was World Cup downhill champion again, beating Ken Read by nine points.

In 1981, he won at Val Gardena but that was all. At Wengen, six weeks after Val Gardena, he was one of two men who might realistically hope to overhaul Canadian Steve Podborski. As he neared the end at Wengen – faster, incidentally, than Podborski would be later – he suddenly lost control and, in what was one of the most horrifying moments of any season, hammered into protective hay bales at full speed. It seemed as if the impact would kill even a strong man but he escaped with a dislocated shoulder.

In 1982 it was a taut thriller right to the end. On Whistler Mountain near Vancouver, Mueller won, with Podborski second; they all went to Aspen for two races and Mueller won them both on successive days but still had to concede the championship to Podborski on a tie breaker. In 1983 he was third at Pontresina, 19th and second at Val Gardena, fourth twice at Kitzbuehel, fourth at Val d'Isere, sixth at Aspen, fourth at Lake Louise.

Cindy Nelson
Ski slalom
Born: August 19, 1955, Duluth, Minnesota, U.S.A.
Height: 5–7. *Weight:* 134.
Career Highlights
Olympic Games: *giant slalom:* 13th, 1980; 21st, 1976; *slalom:* 11th, 1980; 13th, 1976; *downhill:* bronze medal, 1976; seventh, 1980.
World Championships: *giant slalom:* 15th, 1978; 16th, 1982; *slalom:* 11th, 1974; 15th, 1978; *downhill:* silver medal, 1982; fifth, 1978; 18th, 1974
World Cup: *overall:* fourth, 1979; fifth, 1982; seventh, 1983; fifth, 1975; eighth, 1976; ninth, 1977; tenth, 1980; 15th, 1974; *giant slalom:* second, 1983; *downhill:* second, 1978; 25th, 1983.

Cindy, along with Tamara McKinney and Christin Cooper, are the core of the most impressive U.S. women's ski team ever to hit the slopes. Cindy was racing as far back as 1972, although a shoulder injury prevented her from competing at the 1972 Sapporo Olympic Games. But in 1974 she won a downhill at Grindlewald, thus putting to an end 11 consecutive victories by the great Annemarie Moser Proell.

She had decided not to go on racing beyond the 1978 World Championships until she broke a leg at Garmisch. *' In the great solitude of hospital I realised what ski-ing and competition meant to my life.'* So she went on. A

Cindy Nelson.

few minutes after finishing joint seventh in the Lake Placid Olympic downhill she decided to race for another season. It was proved a good decision by her second in a World Cup downhill at Schruns the next year. In 1982, she was generally in the top ten in the downhill and giant slalom.

Some highlights of 1983: a fourth place in a giant slalom at Verbier, a victory in another race there the next day, a tenth at Megeve, a third at Waterville Valley, and second at Vail.

but a long, long way away! The Finnish coaches won't tamper with any of it, for fear of spoiling what natural talent exists already.

He came to prominence in the 1982 season. At 19, he won the 1983 Four Hills tournament (Obertsdorf, Garmisch, Innsbruck and Bischofshofen). He does 2,500 jumps a year on a synthetic arena as well as snow, which means he can practise all the summer.

Christian Orlainsky.

Matti Nykaenen
Ski jumper
Born: July 17, 1963, Juvaeskulae, Finland.
Height: 5–7.   *Weight:* 117.
Career Highlights
World Championships: gold medal, 1982.
Junior World Championships: gold medal, 1981.

Nykaenen, the youngest ever World Champion in 1982, is the leader of the new wave in ski jumping who have brushed aside the men who dominated the sport for so long. Nykaenen is not a jumper, he's a flyer.

Max Golser, who coached the great Austrians, says crisply: *'He's started a new era in ski jumping. You see no power while he jumps, you see no fight with the air or the winds. He is just sailing through the air. It's all so easy, so sure – so aerodynamic.'* And in a more telling expression of admiration, Toni Innauer – for a long time the best in the world alongside Walter Steiner – says: *'His feeling for flying was born in him.'*

Because of his build, he doesn't need a tremendous surge before take off, doesn't need to pitch himself high into the air. His left ski is mostly higher than the right and he can land stiffly –

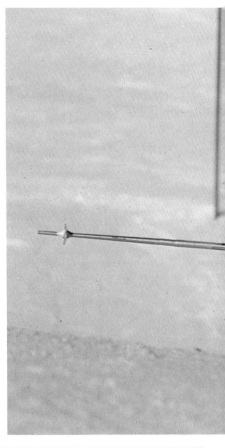

Christian Orlainsky
Ski slalom
Born: February 17, 1962, Tschagguns, Austria.
Height: 5–9. *Weight:* 149.
Career Highlights
Olympic Games: *giant slalom:* 13th, 1980.
World Championship: *giant slalom:* 15th, 1982.
World Cup: *overall:* tenth 1981; 15th, 1983; 17th, 1980; *giant slalom:* 23rd, 1982, 1983; *slalom:* tenth, 1983; 12th, 1982.

Orlainsky is not at the top yet, but he is going in the right direction. His best results in 1982 were a fifth at Garmisch in a slalom and a fifth at Kranjska Gora in a giant slalom. In 1983 he was closing in on the leaders in the slalom, second behind Ingemar Stenmark at Kitzbuehel and a third at Markstein. In the giant slalom: tenth at Val d'Isere.

Brian Orser.

Brian Orser

Singles figure skater
Born: December 18, 1961,
Penetanguishene, Ontario, Canada.
Height: 5–7. *Weight:* 130.
Career Highlights
World Championships: bronze medal
1983; fourth 1982.
Canadian Championships: gold medal
1981, 1982, 1983.
Skate Canada: second 1981, 1982.
St. Ivel: winner 1982.

Orser is known for his superb jumping ability, including his famous triple Axel. He has also improved his compulsory figures, although he was fifth in them at Skate Canada in Kitchener, Ontario in October 1982. (behind Brian Boitano of the United States). He was 1983 Canadian Champion in Montreal (beating Gary Beacom). These should have given him the foundation for a good result in the 1983 World Championships, because Orser's long programme is both technically difficult and full of exciting content. He skates it consistently and earned his first perfect mark of 6.0 at Montreal. For artistic impression he earned 5.9 from all the judges.

But at the 1983 Worlds in Helsinki, he was placed eighth in the figures which, even under the new system of scoring, gave him a mountain to climb. He was second in the short programme and second in the free skating, which put him in third place overall for a bronze medal, a position better than the year before at Copenhagen (when he was beaten by fellow Canadian Brian Pocker – now retired). In the free, Orser did five triples – among them the Axel and flip – and two of the judges actually placed him in front of the winner, Scott Hamilton. He lists his hobbies as ski-ing, reading and playing squash.

Katrien Pauwels

Singles figure skater
Born: November 8, 1965, Ghent, Belgium.
Height: 5–4. *Weight:* 102.
Career Highlights
World Championships: 15th, 1983; 30th 1982.
World Junior Championships: 12th 1982.
European Championships: 15th 1983; 21st 1982.
Belgian Championships: gold medal 1982.
Golden Spin of Zagreb: third 1982.

It's always hard to judge the life and times of any figure skater who comes from a country without a great tradition in the sport. So much of skating is an inheritance, knowledge being passed on from generation to generation, and reputations counting for a great deal. If you're a Carlo Fassi or a Stanislav Zhuk and you present a skater, people have a sense of anticipation. If you're from Belgium, with virtually no background of success, it's not so easy to make it to the top.

In spite of that, Katrien Pauwels is making progress. She got into the women's 'A' final (the competition was controversially split into two finals) in the European Championships at Dortmund in 1983, by virtue of finishing 14th in the compulsory figures and the short. She was 15th out of 16 in the 'A' final, beating only the Czech Hana Vesela. In the World Championships at Helsinki she was last in the 'A' final – 15th out of 15 (12th in the compulsory figures, 20th in the short programme, 15th in the free).

She skates less in training than most others – 17 hours a week in summer, 15 in winter, and enjoys playing the piano, listening to music and dancing jazz ballet.

Perrine Pelen.

Perrine Pelen
Ski downhill
Born: July 3, 1960, Boulogne-
Billancourt, France.
Height: 5–4.   *Weight:* 110.
Career Highlights
Olympic Games: *giant slalom:* bronze
medal, 1980.
World Championships: *giant slalom:*
eighth, 1978; 19th, 1982; *slalom:*
fourth, 1978.
World Cup: *overall:* fourth, 1980; sixth,
1978, 1981; seventh, 1977; eighth,
1982; ninth, 1979; 16th, 1983; *giant
slalom:* second, 1980; sixth, 1982;
ninth, 1981; *slalom:* first, 1980; third,
1981; fifth, 1982.

In 1980, Pelen became the fifth
Frenchwomen to take the World Cup
slalom title, and it meant that France
had won seven of the 14 contested
since 1967. When she began in 1977,
she was immediately noted for her
aggression and technical expertise. But
1980 was the year – a bronze medal in
the giant slalom at Lake Placid even
though she fell on the first run. She did
not finish the slalom at the Olympics,
however. In the World Cup competition
that year, she had a barnstorming
season, with victories in the slalom all
over the place.

She could not maintain that in 1981
(third overall in the slalom), although
she did win at Bormio and Altermarket.
She had been second in the giant
slalom in the season 1980, but fell away
to ninth place in 1981.

Nor was 1982 so happy – fifth in the
slalom and sixth in the giant slalom. In
the second slalom race of the 1983
season at Davos, she was up to third,
then second at Piancavallo, but the rest
of the season seemed to go wrong. In
the giant slalom, she was 13th at Val
d'Isere, tenth at Verbier, eighth at Vail
and ninth at Furano.

Roberto Pelizzola
Ice dancer
Born: October 13, 1958, Milan, Italy.
Height: 5–6.   *Weight:* 136.
Career Highlights
World Championships: 11th 1983.
European Championships: eighth
1983; 11th 1981 (with Elisabetta
Parisi); 13th 1982.
Italian Championships: gold medal
1982.

See **Isabella Micheli**

Mark Pepperday
Singles figure skater
Born: November 15, 1961, Selston,
England.
Height: 5–8.   *Weight:* 126.
Career Highlights
World Championships: 20th 1983; 21st
1982.
European Championships: 14th 1981;
15th 1983; 16th 1982.
European Junior Championships:
silver medal 1977.
British Championships: gold medal
1982, 1983.
St. Ivel: sixth 1982.

Mark Pepperday has had one of the
most unenviable tasks in British sport:
to follow Robin Cousins in men's figure
skating. But, unfortunately, he simply
does not have Cousins' magic nor anything approaching it.

He actually left the sport in 1981
because he wanted to join an ice show,
didn't succeed and returned for the
British Championships at Richmond in
December 1981, where he beat
Christopher Howarth. He reached 16th
place in the 1982 European Championships and a year later 15th. In the
World Championships where the depth
of competition obviously increases, he
was 21st in 1982 and 20th in 1983 –

Mark Pepperday.

21st after the compulsory figures, 19th in the short programme and 20th in the free skating, where he fell doing a triple.

He trains at Nottingham with Wendy Paton. Before the 1983 Europeans, he competed in Skate America at Lake Placid (13th), Skate Canada at Kitchener (tenth) and the Ennia Challenge Cup, and the St. Ivel International when he was sixth. Perhaps the real tragedy of Pepperday is that at moments during free skating he has promised so much, but never been able fo fulfil it.

.

Veronica Pershina

Pairs skater
Born: April 5, 1966, Moscow, U.S.S.R.
Height: 5–0.   *Weight:* 92.
Career Highlights
World Championships: fifth 1983; sixth 1982.
European Championships: fourth 1982, 1983.
U.S.S.R. Championships: silver medal 1983.

Muscovites Veronica Pershina and Marat Akbarov – he's skated since 1968, she since 1972 – were originally trained for pairs skating by Stanislav Zhuk, but by Dortmund and the European Championships in 1983, Zhuk had been mysteriously replaced as coach by Irina Rodnina. Rodnina, of course, is one of the great figures of pairs skating.

Pershina and Akbarov had skated well in the Soviet Championships, but couldn't recapture that at Dortmund, although the Soviet judge marked them higher than the winners, Sabine Baess and Tassilo Thierbach of East Germany. In the short programme, in fact, they had three second places, three thirds and two fourths from the

judges as well as that first. In the free skating Veronica fell on a throw double Axel and made a lot of other mistakes, so they slipped from third after the short to fourth overall. Veronica was only 16 at the time and the pair were clearly nervous.

In the World Championships a month later, they were sixth in the short programme and fifth in the free for an overall fifth place.

Marina Pestova

Pairs skater
Born: December 20, 1963, Sverdlovsk, U.S.S.R.
Height: 4–10.   *Weight:* 88.
Career Highlights
Olympic Games: fourth 1980.
World Championships: silver medal 1982; sixth 1983.
European Championships: silver medal 1982.
U.S.S.R. Championships: gold medal 1983.

The Soviet pair of Marina Pestova and Stanislav Leonovich have had many fitness problems. They missed the whole 1981 season, because of an injury to Marina, and the 1983 European Championships, when she had to have a foot operation.

The pair are coached by the famous Stanislav Zhuk, an agreeable bear of a man who formerly advised the immortal Irina Rodnina and Alexander Zaitsev. In training, Pestova and Leonovich lay stress on the artistic harmony of their composition. Solo dancers of the Moiseev dancing company have worked with them, giving their skating a most distinctive style.

After missing the 1981 season, they went to Copenhagen for the 1982 World Championships, where they were second in the short programme and second in the free skating to take the silver medal. Clearly, missing the 1983 European Championships hampered them for the 1983 Worlds in Helsinki, where they could finish only fourth in the short programme and seventh in the free. But they have a lot going for them: first Zhuk himself, the kingmaker of pairs skating (since 1965 Russians have been absolutely dominant and won every world championship except two); second, the fact that Marina weighs only 88 pounds and so can be lifted easily; third, the facility and back up to train six days a week.

They both enjoy playing tennis.

Marina Pestova and Stanislav Leonovich.

Nicholas Phipps
Bobsleigh
Born: April 8, 1952, London, England.
Height: 6–0.   *Weight:* 202.
Career Highlights
World Four-man Championships:
    ninth, 1981.
British Four-man Championships: gold
    medal, 1979, 1980; silver medal,
    1983.

A physical training instructor, Phipps
joined the British Bobsleigh Association in 1979 after an eight year career
as an international decathlete – he competed in more than 52 of them. Since
coming over to bobs, he has crammed a
lot into a short space of time; so much,
in fact, that he has no time for other
hobbies. He has both driven and acted
as brakeman.

Pavel Ploc
Ski jumper
Born: June 15, 1964, Harrachow,
    Czechoslovakia.
Height: 5–7.   *Weight:* 135.
Career Highlights
World record jump of 181 metres, 1983.
World Cup event winner at Harrachow,
    1983.

Ploc comes from a sporting family: his
father was Czech biathlon champion
many times, his younger brother
Thomas skis, his kid sister Veronica
skis cross country – but at the start of
1983 Pavel was considered just another
promising   Czech   ski   jumper.
Immediately he got the wrong sort of
publicity. At Obertsdorf in Bavaria he
was one of three jumpers disqualified –
he wore advertisements which were too
big on his gloves. But he improved
week by week and won a World Cup
event at Harrachow a month before the
World Championships.

He actually began as a Nordic combined skier (cross country over 15
kilometres, a 70 metre jump) but concentrated, wisely, on jumping. He is
one of the new type of competitors –
called 'milkyfaces' – who dominated
1983: for 'milkyfaces' read schoolboy
looks.

Steve Podborski
Ski downhill
Born: July 25, 1957, Don Mills,
    Ontario, Canada.
Height: 5–8.   *Weight:* 162.
Career Highlights
Olympic Games: *downhill:* bronze
    medal, 1980.
World Championships: *downhill:* ninth,
    1982.
World Cup: *overall:* eighth, 1982; ninth,
    1981; 30th, 1980, 1983; *downhill:*
    first, 1982; second 1981; eleventh,
    1983.

This grandson of a Ukranian farmer
who emigrated to Ontario is one of the
outstanding downhillers in the world.
He started racing when he was ten and
had reached the Can-Am team by
1973. But the big leap – to the World
Cup circuit – was more difficult and he
started slowly in season 1974-75
because of illness and injury. He pro-
gressed in 1976, but then was injured
in the pre-Olympic downhill and
required knee surgery.
  In 1977 he was Canadian downhill
champion, winning his first race –
Morzine. Team-mate Ken Read had a
faster time, but was disqualified
because he wore an illegal race suit. In
1979, Steve was consistent:
9,10,2,7,8,38,8 and that paid off in
1980 when he finished ninth in the
overall downhill and got a bronze medal
in the Lake Placid Olympics.
  By 1981 he was ready to storm the

Steve Podborski (right) being interviewed for television.

citadels of ski racing. He announced his intention with a third at Val d'Isere and a third at Val Gardena before notching a hat-trick of victories at St. Moritz, Garmisch, and Kitzbuehel. Podborski was close to becoming the first North American to win the World Cup downhill title: the victory at Kitzbuehel meant only a couple of other racers, Harti Weirather and Peter Mueller, could rob him.

The end of the season was tight and dramatic. He was third at Wengen, third at St. Anton. The ski circus went off to Aspen for two races. In the first, Weirather was second, Podborski tenth. Weirather now led overall by five points. The season turned on the second Aspen race the following day, Weirather was faster by a fraction – and Podborski had to wait until the next season.

He was fourth at Val D'Isere, fourth at Val Gardena, won at Crans Montana, was second at Kitzbuehel, won a second race there, won at Garmisch, was second at Mount Whistler in Canada. The circus was back at Aspen for the last two races, but this time it was all different. Weirather needed to win both to catch him. In fact Weirather was second and fourth, and Switzerland's Peter Mueller won both races. He and Podborski had 115 points, but Podborski won the tie-breaker because Mueller had had a lowly sixth place at Kitzbuehel. *The only thing I want to do when I go fast is go faster*, says Podborski. He's small for a downhiller, but as he judges it, being lighter he can turn better.

1983 ended badly. At Aspen, his skis stabbed the snow, injuring his left knee and for a time he was reported as considering retirement. Before the injury he had finished 12th at Pontresina, 24th and 17th in the two races at Val Gardena, then second at Kitzbuehel in the famous Hahnenkamm, ninth in another race at Kitzbuehel. He abandoned in one race at Val d'Isere, was 34th in the second, was second at Sarajevo and fourth at St. Anton before Aspen and agony.

Peter Popangelov
Ski slalom
Born: January 31, 1959, Samokov, Bulgaria.
Height: 5–8. *Weight:* 158.
Career Highlights
Olympic Games: *slalom:* sixth, 1980.
World Championships: *giant slalom:* 12th, 1978.
World Cup: *overall:* 13th, 1978, 1980; *slalom:* 16th, 1983.

Now that ski racing is truly international and no longer the exclusive domain of Alpine countries, surprising results do not surprise quite so much. But on January 8, 1980, Popangelov won a slalom at Langgries in West Germany and a Soviet racer, Alexander Zhirov was second. John Samuel captured the mood of the moment when he wrote in the book *Ski Sunday: 'The wind that sprang from the East is now a Force Seven gale.'* At the Lake Placid Olympics a month later Popangelov got himself down the slalom course on Whiteface Mountain in a total time of 1 min. 45.40 secs. to claim sixth place. 1981 wasn't so happy, except for a second place in a World Cup slalom at Garmisch. Nor was 1982 – he made the top ten only once, at Bad Wiessee.

Form guide for 1983: 12th at Madonna, abandoned second run at Parpan, tenth at Kitzbuehel, 11th at

Peter Popangelov.

Kranjska Gora, ninth at St. Anton, tenth at Markstein and seventh at Tarnaby. The question is: has the gale force wind blown itself out?

Mike Pugh
Bobsleigh
Born: July 20, 1953, Wareham, Dorset, England.
Height: 5–10. *Weight:* 168.
Career Highlights
British Four-man Championships: bronze medal, 1983.
British Junior Championships: gold medal, 1981.

This captain in the Royal Tank Regiment says he has financed his team on a bank overdraft. *'I'd rather be poor and successful than rich and never have tried.'*
Apart from bobbing, he likes squash, Rugby and athletics – *'anything that gets the adrenalin going.'* He has competed in the World and European Championships since 1977 and was at Lake Placid for the 1980 Winter Olympic Games.

Maria-Rosa Quario
Ski slalom
Born: May 24, 1961, Milan, Italy.
Height: 5–3. *Weight:* 121.
Career Highlights
Olympic Games: *slalom:* fourth, 1980.
World Championships: *giant slalom:* 12th, 1982; *slalom:* fifth, 1982.
World Cup: *overall:* tenth, 1982; 13th, 1979; 14th, 1983; *slalom:* third, 1983; fourth, 1982; *giant slalom:* tenth, 1982.

Maria-Rosa has been making steady progress. She was fourth in the World Cup slalom in 1982 (and tenth in the giant slalom).

But in 1983 she moved up a place in the slalom. Her season: fourth at Limone Piemonte, a second place at Schruns, then victories at Les Diablerets and Vysoke Tatry, Czechoslovakia.

Urs Raber
Ski downhill
Born: November 28, 1958, Wilderswil, Switzerland.
Height: 5–6. *Weight:* 169.
Career Highlights
Olympic Games: *downhill:* 18th, 1980.
World Cup: *overall:* 15th, 1983; *downhill:* fifth, 1983; 25th, 1981, 1982.

Raber's improvement can be clearly seen in his season-by-season record, particularly 1982-1983: and what happened then is worth plotting in some detail. In the first race at Pontresina he started 19th and came tenth, in the two races at Val Gardena he was fourth and third, and all this before Christmas. On New Year's day he was third at Kitzbuehel and the next day second; at Val d'Isere sixth, at Sarajevo seventh, at Aspen seventh, at Lake Louise ninth. It was a magnificent series of placings and clearly marks Raber as a man to be watched.

Ken Read
Ski downhill
Born: November 6, 1955, Ann Arbor, Michigan, U.S.A.
Height: 5–10. *Weight:* 169.
Career Highlights
Olympic Games: *downhill:* fifth, 1976.
World Cup: *overall:* 11th, 1978, 1980; 22nd 1979; 23rd, 1983; *downhill:* eighth, 1983.

Ken Read was born in the United States, but is a Canadian citizen living

Maria-Rosa Quario.

Ken Read.

in Calgary. He started ski-ing when he was three and competed in Europe as long ago as 1972-73, when he won the Swiss Romande Region Championship.

He joined the Canadian World Cup squad in 1975. And in the first race of the season this doctor's son got himself down Val d'Isere's famous course in 2 mins. 4.97 secs. to become the first Canadian man to win a World Cup race. Canadians were also fourth, ninth, tenth and 13th. As one of them, Dave Irwin, observed: *'This has blown the whole big-time ski world wide open.'* From nowhere, Canada had become a major force in the sport and Read – a quiet, intensely polite, good looking man – was to keep it that way. He says: *'The elite of downhill racing are often viewed as a group of daredevils. In fact they are highly trained competitors with a keenly developed sense of calculated risk: when and where to push to the limit to shave those extra hundreths of seconds; when to respect the speed and the race course.'* They are the words of a man who knows what he's doing.

In season 1980 he won both the classic races – at Kitzbuehel and Wengen. A season later at Garmisch he fell at 80 miles an hour, breaking his nose and tearing knee ligaments. He was back in 1982 and never very far away: fifth, third, third, third. He was back again in 1983, but said he was retiring at the end of it. His record in 1983: sixth at Pontresina, fifth and seventh at Val Gardena; 13th and third at Kitzbuehel, fourth and second at Val D'Isere, fifth at Sarajevo, 11th at Aspen.

His place in downhill folklore is assured: he was the man who proved, at Val d'Isere, you don't have to be born in the Alps to win.

Erwin Resch
Ski downhill
Born: March 4, 1961, Tamsweg,

Erwin Resch.

Austria.

Height: 5–8.   *Weight:* 154.

Career Highlights

World Championships: *downhill:* bronze medal, 1982.

World Cup: *overall:* 12th, 1982; 25th, 1983; *downhill:* fourth, 1983.

Whatever Erwin Resch does with the rest of his career, he will always be known in Britain as the man who prevented their own Konrad Bartelski from winning a World Cup downhill. Resch, a handsome, trim man, had started his career in 1979, finishing a modest 63rd in the overall World Cup standings. The next year he was accelerating, 42nd overall; and in 1982, 12th – and going well. The ski circus moved to Val Gardena in the Dolomites, famous for its camel bumps – three jumps close together. Resch seemed to have given the performance of his life with a time of 2 mins. 7.41 secs. over the 3,446 metre course, beating two Olympic champions – Stock and Klammer – and Podborski, Wirnsberger, Weirather.

As is normal, his victory was being celebrated when Bartelski set off at 29th on the start list. He was a fraction faster than Resch at the first point where times are recorded for all racers, held that to the second time point and lost it only on the bottom part of the course to be second. On the podium, Bartelski smiled broadly, Stock (third) also smiled broadly and Resch looked the way people look when they have avoided a car crash. Resch emphasised his emergence as a leading downhiller by claiming third place in the Schladming World Championships in 1982, a mere fifteen hundredths of a second behind Cathomen of Switzerland. He hoisted fellow Austrian Weirather – the winner – up onto his shoulders to celebrate the victory.

That season in the World Cup . he was to have a fourth at Kitzbuehel and a second at Wengen. And in 1983 he powered into second place at Val Gardena and followed that with a win at Val d'Isere 1 min. 59.26 secs. against Peter Luescher's 1:59.44.

Anne-Flore Rey
Ski slalom

Born: February 2, 1962, La Tronche, France.

Height: 5–4.   *Weight:* 103.

Career Highlights

Olympic Games: *giant slalom:* 25th, 1980.

Anne-Flore Rey.

World Championships: *giant slalom:*
17th, 1982; *slalom:* 20th, 1982.
World Cup: *overall:* 20th, 1983; *giant
slalom:* eighth, 1983.

Rey is making good progress with her
speciality the giant slalom and is certainly a name to watch.

Mark Rowsom
Pairs skater
Born: April 15, 1959, Tilbury, Ontario,
Canada.
Height: 5–2. *Weight:* 150.
Career Highlights
World Championships: ninth 1983.
Canadian Championships: silver medal
1983.
Skate America: fourth 1982.

See **Cynthia Coull**

Manuela Ruben
Singles figure skater
Born: January 14, 1964, Frankfurt,
West Germany.
Height: 5–5. *Weight:* 119.
Career Highlights
World Championships: eighth 1983;
13th 1981; 15th 1982.
European Championships: fourth
1983; tenth 1981; 14th 1982.
West German Championships: gold
medal 1982, 1983.
St. Gervais and Nebelhorn Trophy:
winner 1982.

The girl from Frankfurt, who has
skated since 1973 and is coached by
Erich Zeller, won the West German
Championships at Mannheim in 1982,
where the defending champion, Karin
Riedeger, was only third. Ruben is – or
rather was – an extremely competent
roller skater, like Claudia Leistner, and
was fourth in the West German Roller

Skating Championships in 1981. She
doesn't even list that among her hobbies now. Instead she goes for swimming and reading.

Although Ruben retained her West
German title in 1983 she was subsequently eclipsed by Leistner in both
the European and World Championships. Known as 'Manoo', she was
sixth in the figures at the Europeans
and also sixth in the short programme;
then went to third in the free programme, with a good triple loop and a couple
of triple toe loops. That all added up to
an overall fourth place.

Worse was to follow in the Worlds:
she was seventh in the figures, tenth in
the short programme and eighth in the
free, a long way adrift at eighth overall.
Leistner took the silver medal. Ruben
is now clearly under threat for the West
German title. She skates 35 hours a
week all year round.

Jozef Sabovcik
Singles figure skater
Born: December 4, 1963, Bratislava,
Czechoslovakia.
Height: 5–7. *Weight:* 130.
Career Highlights
World Championships: sixth 1983;
16th, 1982.
European Championships: silver medal
1983; eighth 1982.
Czechoslovakian Championships: gold
medal 1980, 1981, 1982, 1983.

This versatile young man – he enjoys
music, dancing, playing tennis, playing
Soccer and reading – is known as Mr
Marlboro because he smokes so much.

He's been skating since 1970 and,
although absolutely dominant within
Czech skating, only really emerged
internationally with a silver medal in
the 1983 European Championships,
where he was second in the compulsory

Jozef Sabovcik.

figures, second in the short programme, but a disappointing fifth in the free skating, having gone into that final section in the lead overall. He had to skate just after West German Norbert Schramm. He said: *'When I saw his free programme and the public reaction I knew that it would be very hard for me to beat him. But I am happy to have won a medal.'*

A measure of his improvement is that, in the Europeans the year before, he had been only seventh in the figures. In the 1983 World Championships he was third in the figures, but ninth in the short programme and fifth in the free skating, for an overall sixth place.

Horst Schoenau
Bobsleigh

Born: April 2, 1949, Waltershausen, East Germany.
Height: 5–9.   *Weight:* 181.
Career Highlights
Olympic Games: *four-man bob:* bronze medal, 1980.
World Championships: *two-man bob:* silver medal, 1981; bronze medal, 1982; *four-man bob:* gold medal, 1978; bronze medal, 1980.
European Championships: *two-man bob:* gold medal, 1978; silver medal, 1982; fourth, 1983; *four-man bob:* silver medal, 1981; bronze medal, 1978, 1979.

Rainer Schonborn

Ice dancer
Born: May 26, 1962, Zweibrucken, West Germany.
Height: 5–10.   *Weight:* 145.
Career Highlights
World Championships: ninth 1983; 14th 1982; 21st 1981.
European Championships: sixth 1983; 11th 1982; 16th 1981.
West German Championships: gold medal 1983; silver 1982.

See **Petra Born**

Norbert Schramm

Singles figure skater
Born: April 7, 1960, Nuremberg, West Germany.
Height: 5–10.   *Weight:* 154.
Career Highlights
World Championships: silver medal 1982, 1983.
European Championships: gold medal 1982, 1983.
West German Championships: gold medal 1979, 1981; silver 1983; bronze 1982.

Norbert Schramm.

Every morning, so the legend goes, Norbert Schramm reports to a military base in Bavaria, where he's doing his national service, for his duties. Every day the order is the same: go skating.

Far from being a simple soldier, Schramm has become a television celebrity in West Germany because of his constant appearances. That's hardly surprising. He has a vivid personality and for three years has been locked in a three-way struggle within his own country for skating supremacy. The other combatants are Heiko Fischer, German Champion in 1982 and 1983, and Rudi Cerne, champion in 1978 and 1980.

Schramm, who has Michael Stylianos, the Briton who helped Torvill and Dean, as his choreographer, can look at what has happened during the struggle with a wry smile if he chooses. At the West German championships at Mannheim in 1982, Cerne led Schramm after the figures, Schramm led after the short programme, but then his flamboyance cost him everything. In the free he went for nine triples and fell three times. He said: 'Everything risked, everything lost.'

In the European Championships at Lyons in 1982, he won (five first places in the free skating), with Cerne fourth and Fischer, reigning German champion, sixth. In the World Championships in Copenhagen, where Fischer didn't compete Schramm was second behind Scott Hamilton, while Cerne was 15th. So in 1983 the struggle began again at the European Championships in Dortmund. Schramm won, with Fischer fourth and Cerne seventh. However, Schramm nearly fell on a triple Lutz in the short programme, but he got a standing ovation after the free. And in the 1983 World Championships, Schramm won a silver medal again – fourth in the compulsory figures, third in the short programme and third in the free when he almost fell twice. Fischer was eighth and Cerne tenth.

Knut Schubert
Pairs skater
Born: September 9, 1958, Berlin, East Germany.
Height: 5–4. *Weight:* 135.
Career Highlights
World Championships: seventh 1982; eighth 1983.
European Championships: bronze medal 1983; fifth 1982.
East German Championships: silver medal 1982.

See **Birgit Lorenz.**

Michael Seibert
Ice dancer
Born: January 1, 1960, Washington, Pennsylvania, U.S.A.
Height: 5–10. *Weight:* 143.
Career Highlights
Olympic Games: seventh 1980.
World Championships: bronze medal 1983; fourth 1981, 1982.
U.S.A. Championships: gold medal 1981, 1982, 1983; silver 1980.
Skate Canada: winner 1980.

See **Judy Blumberg**

Fabienne Serrat
Ski slalom
Born: July 5, 1956, Bourg d'Oisans, France.
Height: 5–5. *Weight:* 134.
Career Highlights
Olympic Games: *giant slalom:* fourth, 1980; *downhill:* 21st, 1976.
World Championships: *giant slalom:* gold medal, 1974; fifth, 1982; sixth,

Fabienne Serrat.

1978; *slalom:* fourth, 1974; fifth, 1978; tenth, 1982; *downhill:* tenth, 1974.

World Cup: *overall;* fourth, 1978; fifth, 1974; sixth, 1980; seventh, 1976; ninth, 1977; tenth, 1981; *giant slalom:* sixth, 1983.

If other women ski racers have star quality, Fabienne has glamour. Her photograph has regularly decorated ski periodicals for a decade, just as she has decorated the slopes with some blistering performances, starting with a vic-tory in the giant slalom –her preferred choice of the three Alpine disciplines – at the World Championships in 1974. That made her an instant star. But in the 1976 Olympic Games at Innsbruck, she was injured before the giant slalom, and felt humiliated. She went to the Lake Placid Olympics looking for revenge. It was not to be. She was fourth in the giant slalom by the agonising margin of one hundredth of a second from another French racer, Perrine Pelen (Pelen, 2:42.41, Serrat, 2:42.42).

Her 1983 formguide in the giant slalom was sixth at Val d'Isere, fifth and eighth in two races at Verbier, fourth at Megeve, 14th at Mont Tremblant, third at Waterville Valley 16th at Vali and second at Furano.

Wendy Sessions
Ice dancer
Born: January 3, 1959, Birmingham, England.
Height: 5–4.   *Weight:* 121.
Career Highlights
World Championships: 11th 1981; 12th 1983; 13th 1982.
European Championships: seventh 1983; ninth 1981, 1982.
British Championships: bronze medal 1980, 1981, 1982.
Obertsdorft: winner 1980.
Skate Canada: fourth 1982.

Wendy Sessions and Stephen Williams are very much the third British couple behind Torvill and Dean, and Barber and Slater. She is a bank clerk, he is a sales representative – presumably with understanding bosses.

They made a good impression at their first European Championships – Innsbruck, 1981 – to be ninth (in fact, ninth in all sections). In 1982 at Skate Canada they had one of their best results, fourth (again all the way through) and at the 1983 European Championships seventh (yes, all the way through). In the 1983 Worlds, they were 12th (11th after the compulsory dances, 12th in the original set pattern, 12th in the free).

They have been coached by Joan Slater, and are now coached by Gladys Hogg and Bobby Thompson. For relaxation she enjoys dancing and music; he likes dancing as well, and going to the theatre.

Jean-Christophe Simond
Singles figure skater
Born: April 29, 1960, Monaco.
Height: 5–7.   *Weight:* 136.
Career Highlights
Olympic Games: seventh 1980.
World Championships: fifth 1982, 1983.
European Championships: silver medal 1982; sixth 1983.

It seems the career of Simond will be like that of Robin Cousins in reverse. While Cousins could never really excel at compulsory figures and put his friends and supporters through agony while he skated them, Simond has established a mastery of them which means that after the first stage of every competition he is in the lead. It is not enough to win gold medals, of course, so that whereas Cousins would storm up in free skating Simond slips away.

As a measure of his mastery in the figures, consider the European Championships in Lyons in 1982. He won all three figures, with marks as high as 4.4. Only two other skaters got a 4.0 at all. He won the figures in the 1982 World Championships, but could do no better than fifth overall. In the 1983 European Championships in Dortmund, he won the figures, drifted to sixth in the short programme and seventh in the free skating. In the 1983 World Championships he won the figures, was fifth in the short programme and seventh in the free.

How much effect a mysterious lung illness has affected him – he was in a sanitorium a couple of years ago, but the exact illness was never diagnosed – is hard to say. His career has been beset by all manner of problems. In 1976 both his legs were paralysed for a short time. He lists his hobbies as skiing and playing tennis.

Jean-Christophe Simond.

Nicky Slater
Ice dancer
Born: April 6, 1958, Liverpool,
  England.
Height: 5–10. Weight: 140.
Career Highlights
World Championships: fifth 1983;
  seventh 1982.
European Championships: bronze
  medal 1983; fifth 1981, 1982.
British Championships: silver medal
  1978, 1979, 1980, 1981, 1982.
St. Ivel: second 1982.
N.H.K. Trophy: winner 1981.
Ennia Challenge Cup: winner 1982.

See **Karen Barber**

Howard Smith
Bobsleigh
Born: September 29, 1956, Bargoed,
  Mid-Glamorgan, Wales.
Height: 6–0. Weight: 191.
Career Highlights
British Two-man Championships: gold
  medal, 1980, 1981.
British Four-man Championships: gold
  medal, 1981, 1982, 1983.

This soldier – he's with the 1st Queens
Dragoon Guards – is a talented all-
round sportsman who enjoys Rugby,
parachuting, mountaineering, golf and
shooting. He has competed extensively
since he joined the British Bobsleigh
Association in 1979, including the
World Championships from 1980. In
1983 he was in the four-man team, led
by Malcolm Lloyd, which beat the team
led by John Deere at the British Championships at Igls, Austria.

Elisa Spitz
Ice dancer
Born: May 17, 1963, Short Hills, New
  Jersey, U.S.A.

Height: 5–0. Weight: 99.
Career Highlights
World Championships: seventh 1983;
  eighth 1982.
United States Championships: silver
  medal 1983; bronze 1982; fourth
  1981.
Skate America: winner 1982.
Skate Canada: winner 1982.

Although Elisa and her partner Scott
Gregory are very much the second
American dance couple behind
Blumberg and Seibert, they had a very
good season in 1982-83. At Skate
America they were locked in combat
with Soviets Elena Garanina and Igor
Zavorin – but won the compulsory dances, the original set pattern and the free
dancing, and were described as 'new
rising stars'. At Skate Canada they won
all sections, too, from Canadians Tracy
Wilson and Robert McCall.

At the 1983 United States Championships in Pittsburg, Alex McGowan
– a Briton living in California and a
noted coach – wrote of them: 'Finishing
second, they opened their free dance with
a snappy Samba leading into an
expressive 'Hernando's Hideaway'
tango, then into a vivacious 'Hoedown'
ending. They have really developed as a
technically capable team in just one
year. They also gained that all important
second spot on the World Team (with
Blumberg and Seibert)'. They moved up
a place at Helsinki, from eighth to
seventh (sixth in the compulsories,
sixth in the original set pattern and
seventh in the free dance).

They are coached by Rod
Ludington and skate 20 hours a week
all the year.

Roswitha Steiner
Ski slalom
Born: June 14, 1963, Radstatt, Austria.

Height: 5–7.   *Weight:* 112.
Career Highlights
World Championships: *giant slalom:*
    tenth, 1982.
World Cup: *overall:* 23rd, 1982, 1983;
    slalom: fifth, 1983.

Roswitha made a quiet debut in the 1980 World Cup, with her best result a 13th place in a giant slalom at Saalbach. In fact she raced only six times. In 1981 she competed in 15 races and finished 11th twice. In 1982 she was getting closer to the leaders – six results in the top ten. Her 1983 form guide (when she concentrated on the slalom) was: sixth at Davos, fifth at Schruns, fourth at Les Diablerets, fourth at Vyksoke Tatry – and then the big breakthrough with a victory at Waterville Valley, New Hampshire, pushing World champion Tamara McKinney into second place on a soggy slope.

Ingemar Stenmark
Ski slalom

Born: March 18, 1956, Josjo, Sweden.
Height: 5–9.   *Weight:* 159.
Career Highlights
Olympic Games: *giant slalom:* gold
    medal, 1980; bronze medal, 1976;
    slalom: gold medal, 1980.
World Championships: *giant slalom:*
    gold medal, 1978; silver medal, 1982;
    ninth, 1974; *slalom:* gold medal,
    1978, 1982.
World Cup: *overall:* first, 1976, 1977,
    1978; second, 1975, 1980, 1981,
    1982, 1983; *giant slalom:* first, 1975,
    1976, 1978, 1979, 1980, 1981;
    second, 1977, 1982, 1983; *slalom:*
    first, 1975, 1976, 1977, 1978, 1979,
    1980, 1981, 1983; second, 1982.

There is a legend that when Stenmark lived in a hamlet called Tarnaby, up near the Arctic Circle, parties of fans used to go in buses and gaze at his

Ingemar Stenmark takes a tumble.

Ingemar Stenmark.

house in awe and sometimes steal stones from his garden as souvenirs. Such is the amazing appeal the ski racer has in Sweden. Some other 'true' stories . . . Stenmark regularly used to beat Bjorn Borg as Sweden's most popular sportsman . . . the results of his races were always announced on SAS flights, wherever the aeroplanes happened to be in the world . . . his successes converted most of the youth of his country from cross country to Alpine ski-ing . . . when he fell in training and was unconscious for ten minutes, the news wiped Sweden's general election off the front pages.

So who is the man who can do these things? He's shy and very quiet, reluctant to be interviewed and somebody once described him as being able to look like "a hunted animal."

In both giant slalom and slalom racing he has been and, still is, one of the great ones. His speciality is winning with a blistering, astonishing second run. Only three men have won the World Cup outright in three consecutive seasons, Phil Mahre, Gustavo Theoni, and Stenmark.

Stenmark has said it helps him race if he gets angry. Then you see it, the ability to be turning and gliding at the same time, each tight twist of the body a natural extension of the last twist, a projection towards the next. In 1983 he tracked Phil Mahre but couldn't catch him. Mahre had had a poor season until the 'white circus' reached North America. Stenmark was on form – he had won three of his last six races. After the first run at Aspen, Colorado, Stenmark stood a mere .13 of a second behind, but for once could not improve on the second run, and Mahre was World Cup champion. As he looks back, Stenmark can find many consolàtions: of his first 128 World Cup races, he won 62. Under the great Olympic

pressure in 1980, he won both slaloms.

Every year there are whispers about his imminent retirement and, of course, it is going to happen one day. When it does, ski racing will be missing a whole dimension. In 1983 in the slalom, he won at Courmayeur, had a second place at Madonna and a win at Kitzbuehel, won at Markstein, and was third at Gallivare. In the giant slalom, he was third at Kranjska Gora, 11th at Garmisch, won at Todtnau, won at Gallivare, was third at Aspen and third at Furano. He now lives in the Residence l'Annonciade, Monte Carlo, as befits a prince of sport.

Leonhard Stock
Ski downhill
Born: March 14, 1958, Zell am Ziller, Austria.
Height: 6–0.   *Weight:* 154.
Career Highlights
Olympic Games: *downhill:* gold medal, 1980.
World Cup: *overall:* second, 1979; twelfth, 1981; *downhill:* 15th, 1983.

Something happened to Leonard Stock when he tramped up Whiteface Mountain one day in 1980. He examined the Olympic downhill course and thought: I like this track, it's a track for a good performance. He had gone to Lake Placid as a reserve in the Austrian team, but was so fast in training that he forced himself in and the reigning World Champion Josef Walcher out. Stock was not one of the mighty names of downhill and went off ninth. *'I knew my run was good round the bends but you cannot tell. You know nothing. So I had to wait for the other racers to come down. One hour passed every moment'.* His time, in fact, was 1 min. 45.50 secs. He waited until number 19 had come down slower – Russian Valeri Tzyganov

– before he sensed he had won it. He judged, correctly, that no racer after Tzyganov was good enough to beat 1:45.50. His immediate reaction: *'For me it was a beautiful thing.'*

It was also an astonishing thing. He had been racing since 1977 and his overall places in the annual World Cup championships – 31st in 77, then 21st, then second in 1979 –were rising up a scale, but few expected the scale to reach the Olympic medal. Subsequently, he hasn't done well: 15th in the World Championships in Schladming in 1982, 11th over the whole season.

He is a country boy and his family run a *gasthof* in Finkenberg, not far from Innsbruck, where he likes to stay quietly, sometimes doing a little hunting. He says: *'I get nervous when I have to sit giving interviews. It's worse than racing.'* All this cannot mask the central question: was that day on Whiteface Mountain one of those golden days – the only day in the man's life – when all the chemistry came exactly right? In 1983, he was eighth at Val Gardena, 12th at Kitzbuehel, tenth at Val d'Isere and then 12th, an encouraging seventh at St Anton and sixth at Lake Louise.

Leonhard Stock with his Olympic gold medal.

Stig Strand
Ski slalom
Born: August 25, 1956, Tarnaby,
Sweden.
Height: 5–7.   *Weight:* 149.
Career Highlights
World Cup: *overall:* 11th, 1983; *slalom:*
second, 1983; tenth, 1982.

Ingemar Stenmark used to lose to
Strand when they were neighbourhood
juniors – both are from the hamlet of
Tarnaby – but once they reached the
World Cup circuit, everything altered.
Stenmark became virtually invincible
while Strand was struggling far down
the rankings. That did not begin to
change until the tail end of the 1982
season, when Strand finished seventh
at Kranjska Gora and eighth at
Montgenevre. The next season, he won
Madonna beating Stenmark and Phil
Mahre. *'I was looking for a place in the
top three'* he said *'but I never thought I
could beat Stenmark and Mahre.'*
　In fact, Stenmark had been fastest
on that first run (50.95 seconds) with
Bojan Krizaj second (51.09), Paolo de
Chiesa third (51.15) and Strand fourth
(51.45). Mahre was fastest on the
second run, but Strand wasn't far
behind him and his combined time was
enough to give him victory. *'I know he
worked hard to win this race,* Stenmark
said. *'He had to train hard and he had to
change his technique.'* Strand said after
his victory that he wanted to christen
his six week old daughter Madonna. All
this was in the midst of an amazing
season for Strand, who was rapidly
becoming one of the best slalomers in
the world. His form went like this:
second at Courmayeur (behind
Stenmark), the victory at Madonna,
seventh at Kitzbuehel, second at Kranjska Gora, 13th and fourth at Markstein, second at Tarnaby, second at
Gallivare, a victory at Furano.

Rosalynn Sumners
Singles figure skater
Born: April 20, 1964, Palo Alto,
California, U.S.A.
Height: 5–0.   *Weight:* 102.
Career Highlights
World Championships: gold medal
1983; sixth 1982.
World Junior Championships: gold
medal 1980.
United States Championships: gold
medal 1982, 1983.
Skate America: winner 1982.
N.H.K. Trophy: second 1982.
Skate Canada: third 1982.

This Californian became World Champion at Helsinki in 1983, winning the
compulsory figures (she'd only hoped
for a place in the top three), finishing
fourth in the short programme and then
winning the free skating. She is a good,
if not a great champion. In fact, in 1982
she went to the World Championships
at Copenhagen as U.S. champion, but
was eclipsed – as was everybody else –
by an inspired performance from fellow
American Elaine Zayak, who, unfortunately, dropped out of the 1983
event with an ankle injury.
　Sumners, who has a variety of
interests, including acting, modelling
and cooking, started off in 1982 by winning Skate America at Lake Placid,
putting together two very polished programmes. Later in October she came
third at Skate Canada behind Vikki de
Vries (U.S.) and Kristina Wegelius
(Finland). At the U.S. Championships
at Pittsburg in February, she skated a
magnificent free programme (though
she fell once) and all nine judges placed
her first above Zayak.
　In the Worlds, Sumners established
an early lead in the compulsory figures,
and was not to be caught, even by the
new star of women's skating, West German Claudia Leistner.

Rosalynn Sumners.

Alexander Svinin
Ice dancer
Born: July 7, 1958, Leningrad, U.S.S.R.
Height: 6–1. *Weight:* 160.
Career Highlights
World Championships: fourth 1983; sixth 1982.
European Championships: silver medal 1983; fourth 1982.
U.S.S.R. Championships: silver medal 1983.

See **Olga Volozhinskaya**

Tassilo Thierbach
Pairs skater
Born: May 21, 1956, Karl-Marx-Stadt, East Germany.
Height: 5–6. *Weight:* 155.
Career Highlights
Olympic Games: sixth 1980.
World Championships: gold medal 1982; silver 1983.
European Championships: gold medal 1982, 1983.
East German Championship: gold medal 1983.

See **Sabine Baess**

John Thomas
Ice dancer
Born: September 5, 1960, Brampton, Ontario, Canada.
Height: 5–5. *Weight:* 147.
Career Highlights
World Championships: tenth 1983.
Canadian Championships: silver medal 1983.
Skate Moscow: eighth 1982.
Zagreb Golden Spin: fourth 1982.

See **Kelly Johnson**

Kay Thomson
Singles figure skater
Born: February 18, 1964, Toronto, Canada.
Height: 5–2. *Weight:* 103.
Career Highlights
World Championships: seventh 1983; eighth 1982.
World Junior Championships: silver medal 1980.
Canadian Championships: gold medal 1982, 1983; silver 1981.
Skate America: fifth 1982.

The girl who likes dancing and tennis is internationally known for her spins and consistent compulsory figures. In the 1983 Canadian Championships she landed a triple Lutz double toe loop –to become one of very few skaters able to perform a clean triple Lutz. Her spins are executed so fast they produce a strong reaction from crowds.

Kay Thomson.

She was second in the Junior World Championships in 1980 and eighth in the 1982 World Championships at Copenhagen – sixth in the compulsory figures, sixth in the short programme, ninth in the free skating.

In 1983 she retained her Canadian title with a barnstorming performance, particularly in the free skating when she did her triple Lutz. She also included a lot of combination jumps. In the World Championships, she was seventh, finishing sixth in the compulsory figures, eleventh in the short programme and sixth in the free.

Jayne Torvill

Ice dancer

Born: October 7, 1957, Nottingham, England.

Height: 5–0½. *Weight:* 98.

Career Highlights

Olympic Games, fifth 1980.

World Championships: gold medal 1981, 1982, 1983; fourth 1980; eighth 1979; 11th 1978.

European Championships: gold medal 1981, 1982; fourth 1980; sixth 1979; ninth 1978.

British Championships: gold medal 1978, 1979, 1980, 1981, 1982; bronze 1977; fourth 1976.

It was an unforgettable moment. Nine marks came up together on a black strip of a scoreboard: all were 5.9. Outside Helsinki Ice Stadium, it was a bitterly cold late afternoon, inside 6,000 Finns waited for the next set of marks – 5.9's were good of course for technical merit, but not exactly immortal. You could hear the silence and it seemed to last a long, long time, probably about 60 seconds. Then it happened all at once. Nine marks for artistic impression came up together and they would echo round the world for days: 6.0 6.0

6.0 6.0 6.0 6.0 6.0 6.0 6.0.

It didn't seem to matter in that moment of deep exultation that those nine marks had been bestowed by judges from Russia, Italy, Switzerland, Japan, the United States, Canada, Austria, Hungary and Great Britain. But on reflection it proved that Torvill and Dean exercise global powers ... where you come from is irrelevant, you fall under their spell straight away. Helsinki 1983 and the World Championships will stand as a monument to them – or will it just be a milestone? It is certain that nobody among the 6,000 gathered at Helsinki had ever seen nine 6.0's before, and probably won't again.

It all started in 1970 when Jayne became British Junior Pairs Champion with Michael Hutchinson and was second in the senior pairs: they became Senior Champions a year later, and in 1972 were 18th in the European Pairs Championships. That year Dean became British Primary Dance Champion with Sandra Elson: in 1974, they were British Junior Dance Champions and sixth in the Senior Championship. In 1975 both Torvill and Dean were looking for new partners and were brought together under Janet Sawbridge. Success didn't take long. In 1976, they won the Sheffield Trophy, the Northern Championships, St. Gervais, were second at Obertsdorf and fourth in the British championships.

By 1978, they were ninth in the European Championships at Strasbourg. At this time he was a policeman on the beat in Nottingham, so busy *'it was a job to grab a meal,'* and she was an accounts clerk. They were skating when they could, sometimes at dawn. They went to the World Championships in Ottawa (where they would be 11th) and something happened which changed everything; they met Betty Callaway in the hotel lift. She had been training foreign couples and had no particular interest in Torvill and Dean, but she remembered Dean had had a cold and asked how he was feeling. He was so painfully shy, she remembers, he hardly replied. She also met Jayne because there was a costume in the changing rooms, clearly left behind, and she thought *'it belongs to that little British girl,* and took it to her. They were significant moments in British sport. She became their trainer and in 1978 – just before Christmas – they got their first 6.0, in the British Championships. They were not to lose the British Championship again in the next five years.

Mrs. Callaway always sensed they had something, though expressing precisely what it was is more difficult. By 1979 they were sixth in the European Championships, by 1980 fourth; and fifth in the Lake Placid Olympic Games.

They had given up their jobs to concentrate on full time skating. Every Olympic year is, in part, a clearing station: people peak at the Olympics and retire, leaving the future to those coming up. In the case of Torvill and Dean it was merely a stepping stone. They went to the European Championships at Innsbruck in 1981 and won. Torvill said then: *'We're not brother and sister, we're a bit more. It's not a marriage, it's not a boy and his girl friend. It's not a courting couple. That's not on our schedule.'* At Innsbruck, Dean remembered how he started. *'My parents wanted me to have an interest. I bought some skates for £15. I'd never seen an ice rink.'*

A month later they won the World Championships in Hartford, Connecticut. At Lyons in the 1982 European Championships, the exercise of global power began. In the compulsory dances, they got three 6.0's in the free

dancing, eight for artistic impression, another three for technical merit: 14 in all. Dean said: *'I felt in a trance.'* In the World Championships at Copenhagen there were 11 marks of 6.0.

By this time they were virtually living in a Bavarian village called Obertsdorf where they had plenty of time on the ice, and plenty of facilities. By this time, too, Dean had matured and at Press Conferences he was answering questions where Torvill had done before.

They unveiled their routine for the 1983 season in the British Championships at Nottingham in November 1982. It was based on *Barnum,* the West End musical which starred Michael Crawford. Dean had had in mind doing something based around a circus theme and he and Torvill went to see Barnum. Crawford peeked round the curtain, recognised them and invited them to his dressing room. *'For me it was a two-way thing,'* said

Jayne Torvill and Christopher Dean.

Christopher Dean and Jayne Torvill await the judges' decision at Helsinki.

Crawford. *'Whereas Barnum apparently inspired them to put it on ice, I was inspired to think that two world champions in their own particular field would take to it like that. I wanted to be completely involved if they and Betty Callaway would let me.'* Crawford helped with the miming and everyone waited to see Torvill and Dean at the 1983 European Championships at Dortmund, but she hurt her shoulder in training – doing a 'levitation' lift. So to Helsinki. Nobody knew how an international panel of judges would react to a circus theme. And then they found out.

Valeri Tzyganov
Ski downhill

Born: October 14, 1956, Monchegorsk, U.S.S.R.
Height: 5–9.   *Weight:* 175.
Career Highlights
World Cup: *overall:* 18th, 1981; 28th, 1980; 39th, 1982. *downhill:* sixth, 1980.

On March 5, 1981, at Aspen, Colorado, the big strong man with a smile full of mischief lurking behind his moustache, shifted the balance of ski power as Canadian Ken Read had done six years earlier. He became the first Russian to win a World Cup downhill. He comes from Monchegorsk, a nickel and copper mining town between the Finnish border and the Barents Sea.

He joined the World Cup circuit in 1980 when the Soviet team were becoming properly organised. He had begun as a slalom racer at 11 but, competing in Yugoslavia, damaged a knee and decided to concentrate on the downhill instead. *'It was frightening then and it's frightening now,'* he says about the downhill.

He competed in the 1980 Olympic giant slalom and from an impossible start number of 72 on the first run hoisted himself up into sixth place, but he made a crucial mistake late on the second run and that was that. So he had to wait until Aspen – one of the

Valeri Tzyganov.

great centres of capitalism – to announce that the Russians were here. His time was 1 min. 52.95 secs., beating Harti Weirather into second place at 1:53.11. Overall in the downhill that season he was to be sixth, but could not maintain it at Schladming for the World Championships in 1982, where he was 18th in the downhill and 17th in the giant slalom. He found consolation: *Four years ago our boys and girls were not so good and everybody laughed at us. Not now.'*

He is a pleasant man, married with a daughter, and likes science fiction and listening to Abba.

Barbara Underhill
Pairs skater
Born: June 24, 1963, Oshawa, Ontario, Canada.
Height: 4–9.   *Weight:* 99.
Career Highlights
Olympic Games: ninth 1980.
World Championships: bronze medal 1983; fourth 1982; seventh 1981; 11th 1980.
World Junior Championships: gold medal 1978.
Canadian Junior Championships: gold medal 1978.
Canadian Championships: gold medal 1979, 1980, 1981, 1982, 1983.

If anybody can break the Soviet and East German stranglehold on pairs skating it must surely be Underhill and Martini, the pleasant couple from Ontario, who, since they won the World Junior Championships in 1978, have been moving closer and closer. At the 1983 World Championships, they finished third behind Soviet and East German pairs, and were then followed by an American pair (the Carruthers) and two more Russians.

He likes windsurfing and cycling,

she likes squash and cross country skiing, an interesting athletic combination for pairs skating. They are known for their dynamic lifts on the ice and triple throw jumps. Significantly the Canadian Skating Association says *Their programmes are well choreographed to highlight both their athletic and artistic qualities.'* They were consistent in the 1983 World Championships, third in the short programme and third in the free skating.

Elena Valova
Pairs skater
Born: January 4, 1963, Leningrad, U.S.S.R.
Height: 5–0.   *Weight:* 103.
Career Highlights
World Championships: gold medal 1983.
European Championships: silver medal 1983.
U.S.S.R. Championships: bronze medal 1982.

Tamara Moskvina, coach to Elena Valova and Oleg Vasiliev is small and full of gentle mischief. There seems to be a factory in the Soviet Union which produces pairs skaters but if you mention that to Tamara she says: *No, factories produce the same thing. Skaters are all different.'* Even by her standards she produced the coup of 1983.

Although Valova and Vasiliev have skated together for only four years and had to miss the 1983 Soviet Championships because Elena was ill, they gave a strong and powerful performance at Skate America in Lake Placid and set off for the European Championships in Dortmund. Russians have a formidable tradition in pairs skating – they say you can pick dozens of good couples from any Moscow or Leningrad rink – and they and the East Germans

Paul Martini and Barbara Underhill.

have dominated the discipline for years. East Germans Sabine Baess and Tassilo Thierbach duly won at Dortmund, but the Russian couple – after being fourth in the short programme – jumped to second place overall with stunning skating.

At the 1983 World Championships, they were second to Baess and Thierbach in the short programme – but poised for greater things. They won the free skating ... and the gold medal. Both like music and Vasiliev enjoys skate-boarding.

Oleg Vasiliev
Pairs skater
Born: November 22, 1959, Leningrad, U.S.S.R.
Height: 5–9.   *Weight:* 157.
Career Highlights
World Championships: gold medal 1983.
European Championships: silver medal 1983.
U.S.S.R. Championships: bronze medal 1982.

See **Elena Valova.**

Elena Valova and Oleg Vasiliev.

Elena Vodorezova.

Elena Vodorezova
Singles figure skater
Born: May 21, 1963, Moscow, U.S.S.R.
Height: 5–2.   *Weight:* 103.
Career Highlights
World Championships: bronze medal,
1983; fifth 1982.
European Championships: silver medal
   1983; bronze 1978, 1982.
U.S.S.R. Championships: gold medal
   1982, 1983.

Elena, trained by the famous Stanislav
Zhuk, was out of skating through illness
for almost four years but, despite that,
easily won the Soviet Championship on
her return to the sport. Her jumping
remained light and weightless, like that
of the ballerinas at the Bolshoi. Interestingly, her main hobby is the produc-
tions of the Bolshoi, and the young solo
dancers there help with her
choreography. *'While in the past
Vodorezova was a kind of amusing child
on ice, today she is an elegant young
woman.'* – says her official biography.
*'Her skating is not an end in itself for
her, but a way of self-expression and a
striving for communication with people.'*

She arrived in skating as that amusing child – somebody used the word
precocious – in 1976 as a 12-year-old at
the World Championships at
Gothenburg and was 11th. After a
bronze medal at the 1978 European
Championships – the best result ever
by a Soviet woman – she developed
arthritis in the knees and did not return
until 1982. At the European Championships in 1983 she won the compulsory figures, was third in the short
programme and fifth in the free, where
she fell on her single attempt at a triple
jump. In the World Championships she
was third in the figures, third in the
short and fourth in the free.

She's skated since 1969 and enjoys
music as well as ballet.

Olga Volozhinskaya
Ice dancer
Born: May 18, 1962, Tallinn, Estonia, U.S.S.R.
Height: 5–7.   Weight: 117.
Career Highlights
World Championships: fourth 1983; sixth 1982.
European Championships: silver medal 1983; fourth 1982.
U.S.S.R. Championships: silver medal 1983.

The trainer of Olga and Alexander Svinin said three years ago: 'This is the only ice dancing duet whom I allow to improvise at high-calibre competitions.' This is certainly a high risk, but it fully justified itself at the World Championships at Hartford in 1981. Olga was then 19 and Alexander was 23. Unfortunately Olga fell ill on the day of the free skating. 'When I woke up in the morning I felt I was too hot,' she said. She had a temperature. They didn't go to the morning training session, but did skate in the competition and finished a creditable fifth.

They began to train together in 1973. Olga was born in Tallinn (Estonia) and Alexander in Leningrad. At the age of 11 he wanted to be an ice hockey player. 'I wielded the stick well enough but my skating was not up to standard,' he recalls. 'So the coach to the children's ice hockey team recommended that I should first train with figure skaters. I followed his advice. A year passed, I got accustomed to the new sport and I did not notice how it had supplanted ice hockey in my heart.'

When he first skated with Olga, they kept falling down. But their coach told them: 'Always remember the main milestones along the road which you are following – here you must support the partner, in this place you should move away, and here you should look round.

When you learn to pass the milestones the falls will stop.' Alexander is reserved and quiet, but with a wicked sense of humour. 'I sometimes forget I must be near Olga and find myself behind her. Olga is doing her utmost whereas I am clinging to her like an empty railway car.'

She says: 'Several years ago we agreed we would never quarrel. Our duties are clearly distributed. Alexander sharpens the skates and I keep the costumes in order. It does not pay to quarrel with him because he is the best cook among the members of the national team.'

Their finest performance so far came in the 1983 European Championships, when they took the silver medal and the British judge Pam Davis marked them above Soviet couple Bestemianova and Bukin in the original set pattern. At the 1983 World Championships, they were fifth after the compulsory dances, fourth in the original set pattern and fourth in the free dancing. She likes ballet and music, he likes music (and, presumably, cooking).

Josef Walcher
Ski downhill
Born: December 8, 1954, Schladming, Austria.
Height: 5–8.   Weight: 166.
Career Highlights
Olympic Games: downhill: ninth, 1976.
World Championships: downhill: gold medal, 1978.
World Cup: overall: seventh, 1978; eighth, 1977; 22nd, 1980; 23rd, 1975; 28th, 1973; downhill: second, 1977, 1978; seventh, 1980; 14th, 1981; 18th, 1982.

The name Josef Walcher should stand as a monument to downhill racing

Josef Walcher.

because it embraces the agony and the ecstasy of the sport. On a January day in 1978, Franz Klammer went for the World Championships downhill and a reported million dollar offer to turn professional if he won. He was joint fifth. Another Austrian, Walcher, beat him. *'It was very strange to have everybody coming to ask me questions. I learned from Franz what to say. For me he was the greatest. Now we are equal.'*

It didn't work out like that, though. Next season he won at Groden, but he could not find consistency – 25, 27, 12, 22, 17, 59 and – significantly – abandoned at the final downhill at Lake Placid, which, all other considerations aside, was at least some sort of form guide to the Winter Olympics to come there in 1980.

The Austrian team boss, Charlie Kahr, is a tough little man who constantly has to make big decisions because he has so many good downhillers. And although Walcher was to finish seventh overall in the final downhill table, he went to the Olympics not sure of his place. Kahr had evidently decided to base his team selection purely on what happened during the training runs and Leonhard Stock got in. Walcher was dropped. He wandered around the bottom of the course after the race looking forlorn and abandoned, murmuring plaintively to himself in broken English: *'I not happy this day.'*

Perhaps that was the effective end of his career. In 1981 he had drifted to 14th in the downhill standings, and in 1982, 18th.

Maria Walliser
Ski downhill
Born: May 27, 1963, Mosnang,
Switzerland.
Height: 5–5. *Weight:* 130.
Career Highlights
World Championships: *downhill:* 12th,
1982.
World Cup: *overall:* fifth, 1983; 12th,
1981; 17th, 1982; *giant slalom:* tenth,
1983; 25th, 1982; *downhill:* second,
1983; eighth, 1982.

It is a bit unfair to describe the girl with
the charming smile as purely a downhill
racer. Her giant slalom has been
improving, although she is not as strong
in this as the downhill. From being
third in both disciplines in the Swiss

Maria Walliser.

Championships in 1981, she has quickly established herself as one of the
best downhillers in the world.

There were signs of what was to
come in season 1982: a tenth at
Grindelwald, then a sixth there, a tenth
and an eighth at Badgastein, a third at
Arosa in her native Switzerland and a
strong finish with a second at Arosa
again. It was a warning to everybody. In
1983 the breakthrough came. At
Megeve in France, she swept
everybody aside. However, there was
almost a freak result. American Maria
Maricich, largely unknown, in her
second season and starting way back at
40th on the list, came up to second
place. Walliser was tenth in another
race at Megeve the next day, fourth at
Les Diablerets, won again at Jahorina
in Yugoslavia, and was second at Mont
Tremblant, Canada, behind a Canadian,
Laurie Graham.

Her hobbies are reading and
knitting.

Kristina Wegelius
Singles figure skater
Born: October 12, 1960, Helsinki,
Finland.
Height: 5–7. *Weight:* 126.
Career Highlights
Olympic Games: tenth 1980.
World Championships: sixth 1981,
1983; ninth 1982.
European Championships: fourth
1979, 1980, 1981; sixth 1982, 1983.
N.H.K. Trophy: winner 1981.
Skate America: third 1982.

Kristina Wegelius has skated since
1966, but never quite reached the top,
as her results demonstrate. In fact the
highlight of her career might well be
regarded as the N.H.K. victory in
Japan in 1981, when she won the short
programme and was second to Vikki de

Kristina Wegelius.

Vries in the free skating.

A year later in the European Championships at Lyons, her consistency took her to within striking distance of a medal in a major championship – again.

Just before Christmas 1982 she went to Skate America at Lake Placid and was a strong third behind World Champion Rosalynn Sumners and West Germany's Claudia Leistner –first in the figures, third in the short and fourth in the free. That might have opened up the way to a good season in 1983, but she made a poor showing at the European Championships in Dortmund, only fifth in the figures where she was expected to win. Worse was to follow. After being eighth in the short programme, she didn't do a single triple in the free programme and so finished sixth overall.

In the World Championships in her home town, Helsinki, she found her touch again in the figures – second behind Sumners – but her free skating was not strong enough to sustain that through the competition and she drifted away to sixth overall. She has been coached by Carlo Fassi, but is now with Pia Saikkonen. She likes classical ballet and jazz ballet.

Harti Weirather
Ski downhill

Born: January 25, 1958, Reutte, Austria.
Height: 5–9.   *Weight:* 158.
Career Highlights
World Championships: *downhill:* gold medal 1982.
World Cup: *overall:* eighth 1981; tenth 1982; 13th 1983; 15th 1980; *downhill:* first, 1981; third, 1982, 1983.

At the end of the World Championship downhill at Schladming he saw his time, raised fists with his ski poles clenched in them and shook them convulsively. It was a moment of the purest intoxication. The farmer's son who likes reading detective stories and science fiction had given plenty of warning of that world title. In 1980-91 he won the World Cup on the last day of the season at Aspen, Colorado, from Canada's Steve Podborski (overall Weirather 115 points, Podborski 110) and on the way to that he had won races at Cortina and St. Anton.

Weirather's career began in 1979 and his immensely strong body was the perfect vehicle for downhill racing. Austria yearned for another God to worship – Franz Klammer was in temporary decline then – and Weirather began to deliver. In 1982, apart from winning the World Championship, he would be quickest at Kitzbuehel and Wengen. Weirather is versatile, enjoys motor sport and water ski-ing and is widely known as a pleasant, polite young man.

Weirather's time at Schladming was 1 min. 55.10 secs. The next quickest was the Swiss, Conradin Cathomen at 1:55.58. As these things go, it was a comfortable margin and there cannot be much doubt that – barring accidents – Weirather must have real chances at Sarajevo in the Olympic downhill. This impression was reinforced over the whole of 1983 when he won at Pontresina, was third at St. Anton, fourth at Aspen and never out of the top dozen. That is consistency.

Andreas Wenzel
Ski slalom

Born: March 18, 1958, Liechtenstein.
Height: 5–7.   *Weight:* 149.
Career Highlights
Olympic Games: *giant slalom:* silver medal, 1980; *slalom:* tenth, 1976;

Andreas Wenzel.

12th, 1980.
World Championships: *giant slalom:* silver medal, 1978; *downhill:* 13th, 1978; *slalom:* 18th, 1978.
World Cup: *overall:* first, 1980; third, 1978, 1983; fifth, 1982; sixth, 1979; seventh, 1981; *slalom:* third, 1983; *giant slalom:* second, 1978.

Although Liechtenstein may be a small place, it has exerted considerable influence on ski racing, mainly through the Wenzels: Andreas and his sisters Hanny and Petra. Andreas won the World Cup in 1980 – and so did Hanny. In fact they both competed in the 1976 Innsbruck Olympics, but Andreas barely revealed a hint of the majestic triumphs to come. At Innsbruck, he was 20th in the giant slalom with a time of 1 min. 48.53 secs., an eternity behind the winner, Heini Hemmi at 1:45.41.

A car accident in 1979 left him momentarily unconscious. And he began the 1981 season after a serious ligament injury in training at Zermatt that kept him out for six weeks.

He wants to be known as a real champion, mastering downhill as well as slaloms. *'I have always been able to prepare myself calmly, in peace, at my rhythm, without making myself anxious,'* he said that year. *'I don't think too far ahead, to concentrate better on the present moment.'* That certainly worked. In 1980 he was fourth in the famous Kitzbuehel downhill, fifth at Lake Louise in the last race of the season; won the slalom at Kitzbuehel, won the giant slalom at Oberstaufen. He had a good Olympic Games too, coming second in the giant slalom behind Ingemar Stenmark.

He had an excellent season in 1983. In the slalom: third at Parpan, fourth and seventh at Markstein, second at St. Anton, a victory at Tarnaby from Stig

Strand and a second to Strand at Furano. In the giant slalom, after a slow start, he was sixth at Adelboden, fourth at Garmisch and fifth at Todtnau.

Hanny Wenzel
Ski slalom
Born: December 14, 1956, Staubirnen, West Germany.
Height: 5–4.   *Weight:* 125.
Career Highlights
Olympic Games: *downhill:* silver medal, 1980; 11th, 1976; *giant slalom:* gold medal, 1980; 20th, 1976; *slalom:* gold medal 1980; bronze medal 1976.
World Championships: *downhill:* 13th, 1974; 29th, 1978; *giant slalom:* fifth, 1978; seventh, 1974; *slalom:* gold medal, 1974; sixth, 1978.
World Cup: *overall:* first, 1978, 1980; second, 1975, 1979, 1983; third, 1974, 1981; fifth, 1973, 1977; ninth, 1976; 19th, 1982.

This is a formidable ski family: Hanny, brother Andreas and sister Petra. Hanny, a confident ski racer who now lives in Liechtenstein, has had an almost extraordinary career. As long ago as 1974 – quite literally a generation away from most present racers – she won the slalom in the World Championships at St. Moritz. In fact she had got her first World Cup points at Heavenley Valley in 1972. Even in 1980, when she'd won the World Cup twice, she said: *'It's important for an athlete to know the future, not to be worried about getting back to a normal life. One day I want to have a family and busy myself around the family hearth, but I want to have lived an active life.'*

The supreme moment came at Lake Placid in the 1980 Winter Olympic Games. *'My second place in the downhill suddenly put me in the right orbit and everything passed as a dream. I admit, however, to being more nervous than I*

Hanny Wenzel.

have ever been before the second run of the giant slalom. But in the slalom I stayed very cold and concentrated very hard. I'm very steady, I don't need to take big risks to get a good time.' In the downhill she clocked 1 min. 38.22 secs. and was beaten only by the great Annemarie Moser-Proell; in the slalom, 1:25.09 against Christa Kinshofer's (West Germany) 1:26.50; in the giant slalom 2:41.66 against Irene Epple's (West Germany) 2:42.12.

The next season she slipped back to third in the World Cup table, without a win all season. She was injured in the summer of 1981 and out of action for most of the next season, returning only for the World Championships, when she failed to finish. But she was back in form in 1983 with a giant slalom win at Furano and a clutch of top ten placings in both slalom and giant slalom.

Petra Wenzel
Ski slalom

Born: November 20, 1961, Planken, Liechtenstein.

Height: 5–2. *Weight:* 114.

Career Highlights

Olympic Games: *slalom:* 14th, 1980. World Championships: *downhill:* 49th 1978; *giant slalom:* fourth, 1982; 29th, 1978.

World Cup: *overall:* 19th, 1983; 25th, 1982; *giant slalom:* 16th, 1983; *slalom:* ninth, 1983.

The third member of the ski racing family from Liechtenstein – Hanny is her sister, Andreas her brother – has not enjoyed their distinguished records, although in the 1977 Swiss National Championships she held out much promise with a fifth place in the slalom. By 1980, while Hanny was mov-

The Wenzel family – Hanny, Andreas and Petra.

Petra Wenzel relaxing at home.

ing from triumph to triumph, Petra was having a much more modest time. Like her sister she was competing in all three Alpine disciplines. Her best result that season was seventh in a giant slalom at Val d'Isere. In 1981, she concentrated on the giant slalom but could not get into the top 15 in any of the nine races.

In 1982, she did much better, ninth at Chamonix, 11th at Badgastein,

eighth at Lengrries before a fourth – which must have seemed like water in a desert – at Berchtesgaden, a fifth at Alpe d'Huez and 11th in Montgenevre. All this was in the slalom, where she finished on 43 points.

In 1983 her best results were a fourth at Maribor and a fifth at Les Diablerets. In the giant slalom, after a mediocre start, she fired in a fifth place at Mont Tremblant.

Stephen Williams
Ice dancer
Born: May 23, 1960, Birmingham, England.
Height: 5–10.   *Weight:* 156.
Career Highlights
World Championships: 11th 1981; 12th 1983; 13th 1982.

European Championships: seventh 1983; ninth 1981, 1982.
British Championships: bronze medal 1980, 1981, 1982.
Obertsdorft: winner 1980.
Skate Canada: fourth 1982.

See **Wendy Sessions**

Wendy Sessions and Stephen Williams.

Tracy Wilson
Ice dancer
Born: September 25, 1961, Port
  Moody, British Columbia, Canada.
Height: 5–2.   *Weight:* 125.
Career Highlights
World Championships: sixth 1983;
  tenth 1982.
Canadian Championships: gold medal
  1982, 1983.
St. Ivel: fourth 1982.
Skate Canada: second 1982.
Ennia Challenge Cup: third 1981.

Tracy and her partner Robert McCall
are trained by England's former champion Bernie Ford . . . and they are making clear progress. At the 1983
Canadian Championships at Montreal,
they won all three compulsory dances
and in the original set pattern were
awarded a perfect mark of 6.0 – and
another in their free dancing.

Wilson can be cryptic when she
chooses. After the 1982 Canadian
Championships, she said: *'The Blues is
a tragic dance. I was spilling my heart
out trying to be sad, but all people said
was that I sure looked sexy. When I tried
to be sexy, it never worked. I don't know,
when I want to look sad, maybe I should
try to be sexy'.* A Canadian journalist
has said that Wilson and McCall
sounds like a firm of accountants.
Never mind. After all, an American
journalist said that Torvill and Dean
sounded like a vaudeville act.

The Canadian pair were only tenth
in the 1982 World Championships, but
took their creative skating to the 1983
Championships and were seventh after
the compulsory dances, a very good
fifth in the original set pattern and sixth
in the free dancing. (That told the story
of a young couple in love before the
war, the changes in mood as the war
breaks out and after the war.)

For relaxation she likes swimming
and dancing; he likes writing, swimming
and music.

Tracy Wilson and Robert McCall.

Peter Wirnsberger
Ski downhill

Born: September 13, 1958, Leoben, Austria.

Height: 5–10. *Weight:* 160.

Career Highlights

Olympic Games: *downhill:* silver medal, 1980.

World Championships: *downhill:* 12th, 1982.

World Cup: *overall:* 16th, 1979; 17th, 1978; 18th, 1981; 19th, 1980; *downhill:* 17th, 1983.

When Charlie Kahr, supremo of the Austrian ski team, decided not to take Franz Klammer to Lake Placid for the Olympic Games, he was so unpopular his house and family had to be guarded. When Kahr got to Placid, he promptly decided not to pick the then World Champion, Josef Walcher, for the downhill. Kahr was saved (perhaps literally) because an Austrian, Leonhard Stock, won the race. It is very easy to forget that another Austrian, Peter Wirnsberger, was second, beaten by only 62 hundredths of a second.

Wirnsberger is noted for his aggression, for what fellow racer Ken Read has termed *'all out attack.'*

He started on the World Cup circuit in 1977 when he was 24th overall; a year later he was up to 17th; then 16th. Inspired perhaps by that downhill at Lake Placid, he was very nearly the man of 1981: second at St. Moritz, third at Kitzbuehel and second at St. Anton. His best performance in 1982 was third at Wengen, although he had a fourth at Crans Montana. He was 12th in the World Championships in Schladming in a not very distinguished season.

In 1983 he was 16th at Sarajevo and 17th in the World Cup.

Peter Wirnsberger.

Janina Wirth
Singles figure skater
Born: December 20, 1966, Berlin, East Germany.

Height: 5–4. *Weight:* 115.

Career Highlights

World Championships: 11th 1983; 12th 1982.

World Junior Championships: gold medal 1982.

European Championships: eighth 1983; ninth 1982.

East German Championships: silver medal 1982.

The year 1982 was a good one for Wirth, who finished second in the East German national championships at Karl-Marx-Stadt to Katarina Witt, the holder. She is not yet ready to offer any challenge to Witt.

In the European Championships at Lyons in 1982 (when Wirth was under age, but allowed to enter because she was World Junior Champion), Witt was second and Wirth ninth (tenth compulsory figures, 18th short programme – a disaster out of 28 competitors – seventh in the free programme).

In the European Championships at Dortmund in 1983, she began to fulfill her promise, up to eighth (tenth in the compulsory figures, fourth in the short, eighth in the free) and she maintained that in the World Championships in Helsinki with an overall 11th place (15th in the figures, seventh in the short, tenth in the free). She lists her only hobby as music.

Katarina Witt
Singles figure skater
Born: December 3, 1965, Karl-Marx-Stadt, East Germany.

Height: 5–4. *Weight:* 113.

Career Highlights

World Championships: silver medal

Katarina Witt.

1982; fourth 1983.

European Championships: gold medal 1983; silver 1982.

East German Championships: gold medal 1982, 1983.

Taught by the formidable Jutta Muller, who also trained the 1980 Winter Olympic Games champion Anett Poetzsch, Katarina Witt can look older than her years. Despite her protege becoming European Champion in 1983 at Dortmund, Muller was quoted as saying: '*I have hardly watched a weaker women's final. There were too many faults and falls.*' Included among those who fell was Witt, on a triple loop. However her superiority over the opposition – of whatever quality – was there for all to see: second in the compulsory figures, first in the short programme, first in the free skating, including a double Lutz – triple toe loop combination.

In the World Championships in Helsinki, she dropped to eighth in the compulsory figures after a mistake on the third figure, the loops, and was given marks as low as 2.7. She was second in the free behind the champion Rosalynn Sumners, although three judges had her ahead of Sumners. That meant fourth place and no medal at all, an extreme disappointment after taking the silver medal in 1982. She enjoys listening to music in her spare time.

Charlene Wong
Singles figure skater
Born: March 4, 1966, Pierrefonds, Quebec, Canada.
Height: 5–2. *Weight:* 102.
Career Highlights
World Championships: 12th 1983.
Canadian Championships: silver medal 1983; fourth 1981; fifth 1982.
Ennia Challenge Cup: fifth 1982.
N.H.K. Trophy: third 1981.
Grand Prix International: winner 1981.
Skate America: fifth 1982.

Charlene Wong is a proficient and consistent figure skater: she portrays a very feminine style in her free skating programmes and has a consistently high double Axel. She combines triple jumps in her free programme with some original moves. She also likes ballet, jazz, reading and the piano.

The 1982-83 season was a point of arrival for her. At Skate America before Christmas she was fifth, showing an artistic long programme. In the Canadian Championships – Montreal, 1983 – she was second, although she had been adrift after the compulsory figures (fifth), but redeemed herself in the short programme with a top-class

combination (double Axel, double toe loop). She couldn't hope for the championship; she made too many mistakes in the free programme for that, although she did land a triple toe loop. But the overall improvement – from fifth in 1982 to second in 1983 – was there for all to see. And she did well for a 17-year-old in her first World Championships in Helsinki in March 1983 – 13th in the compulsory figures, eighth in the short programme, 11th in the free for 12th place.

Jim Wood
Biathlete
Born: October 13, 1952, Sherborne, Dorset, England.
Height: 5–7. *Weight:* 174.
Career Highlights
British Championships: *20 kilometres:* gold medal, 1981.

Biathletes are cross country racers who carry rifles on their backs. They have to ski and, at certain intervals, shoot at targets. It is merciless. It started as bear hunting on skis. John Moore, Director of the British team says: *'The enormous physical effort of skiing compared with the calm concentration required during shooting has produced the perfect test of the athlete.'*

Jim Wood is an experienced member of the British team. But his opponents are formidable – Frank Ullrich of East Germany won the 10 kilometres at Lake Placid and was second in the 20 kilometres. Of the nine medals, eight were taken by East Germany and the U.S.S.R.

Karen Wood
Figure skater
Born: July 15, 1962, Gateshead, Tyne and Wear, England.

Height: 5–6. *Weight:* 114.
Career Highlights
World Championships: 15th, 1981;
17th, 1982.
European Championships: eighth,
1982; 11th 1981.
British Championships: gold medal,
1983; silver 1981.

Karen came to prominence in 1981
when she was locked in a duel with
Debbie Cottrill (now professional) for
the British title. Unfortunately she had
to spend most of 1982 recovering from
an operation on her knees. But in
November 1982 she entered the Ennia
Cup in The Hague and was seventh
(ninth in the short programme, sixth in
the free). As a test to see if her knees
could take the strain, it was a success.
She went on to regain her British title
at Solihull in December and travelled
to the European Championships in
Dortmund. What happened there is
shrouded in mystery. Complaining of a
heavy cold, she was a disappointing
15th after the compulsory figures, making a mess of the first figure. Then she
was only 16th in the short programme
and the doctor put her on antibiotics,
which meant she could not compete in
the free section, but might have been fit
for the World Championships in
Helsinki in March. Instead she was
dropped from the team for Finland for
disciplinary reasons.

Jonathan Woodall
Bobsleigh
Born: January 25, 1946, Oxford,
England.
Height: 6–5½. *Weight:* 217.
Career Highlights
Olympic Games: *four man:* tenth 1980;
two man: ninth 1980.
World Cup: *four man:* bronze medal
1983.

British Four-man Championship: gold
medal 1980, 1981.
British Two-man Championship: gold
medal 1980.

Major Woodall drives with Tony
Wallington, Bob Wootton and Peter
Lund.

Elaine Zayak
Singles figure skater
Born: April 12, 1965, Paramus, New
Jersey, U.S.A.
Height: 5–0. *Weight:* 105.
Career Highlights
World Championships: gold medal

Elaine Zayak.

1982; silver medal 1981.
United States Championships: gold medal 1981; silver 1983; bronze 1982.
St. Ivel: winner 1982.

There is a memory of the 1983 World Championships in Helsinki which won't go away: Zayak, the defending champion, leaving the Myyrmaki rink after only two of the compulsory figures in tears, banished from the competition because of an ankle injury. Thus was gone – all in a moment – the great surprise packet of the sport.

Despite having a mangled left foot – an electric lawn mower ran over it when she was two and a half – she became a 'jumping machine' rifling out triple jumps as if they came from a machine gun. She describes, cryptically no doubt, her special moves as 'just triple jumps.'

It is this ability more than anything else which has enabled her to surge from far back and destroy all opposition, as she did in the 1982 Worlds, when she was fourth after the figures, a disastrous tenth in the short programme and then swept – or rather leapt – to first place in the free; one of the most astonishing reversals of all time in a sport famous for its orderly progressions.

She went back to Paramus, New Jersey, and they put up a plaque just beneath the town sign, which announced that the world champion lived there. Heady stuff. In fact, she is coached by an Englishman, Peter Burrows, who has coined a phrase famous for its masterly understatement. While Zayak was making her way in the sport, he'd eye a competition and say: 'I think we might do well there.' An American journalist has equated this with saying: Let's go and sink the Bismark.

But in the 1983 United States Championships at Pittsburg, she was fourth after the figures and couldn't get up beyond third place in the short programme. She skated first in the final group in the free and made only one mistake – a hand down on the ice: but in her programme was the full armoury of jumps. Rosalynn Sumners (who would become World Champion in Helsinki after Zayak had taken the plane home) responded with a superb performance and all nine judges placed her above Zayak. Then at Helsinki Zayak didn't do well in the first two compulsory figures and was 11th – her assistant coach Mary Lyn Gelderman had said: 'If she comes through the compulsories tenth or lower, there's just no way she can pull this off.' It didn't matter . Her ankle swelled and she could only turn outwards on skates. So she went home, saying: 'I'll be back for the Olympics.'

Daniela Zini
Ski slalom
Born: May 30, 1959, Livigno, Italy.
Height: 5–2.   *Weight:* 112.
Career Highlights
Olympic Games: *slalom:* seventh, 1980.
World Championships: *giant slalom:* seventh, 1982; 34th, 1978; *slalom:* bronze medal, 1982; 11th, 1978.
World Cup: *overall:* ninth, 1980; 11th, 1981; 14th, 1979; 27th, 1983; *giant slalom:* 25th, 1983; *slalom:* ninth, 1983.

Daniela has never quite reached the summit of ski racing, although she has been close. In 1979 she was in the top ten in slalom five times. She improved on that in 1980, and in 1981 she was second twice. The frustration continued in 1982 with just one second place in the World Cup event at Alpe

Daniela Zini.

d'Huez, but there was a World Championship bronze medal to compensate. She started 1983 with a fifth at Limone, then abandoned in the next three races before she finally got down a course at Les Diablerets in eighth place. She was fifth at Maribor, sixth at Vysoke Tatry and ninth at Waterville Valley and Furano. In the giant slalom, her best results were inside the top 15, but not much more.

Pirmin Zurbriggen
Ski giant slalom
Born: February 4, 1963, Saas-Almagell, Switzerland.
Height: 5–9. *Weight:* 165.
Career Highlights
World Cup: *overall:* sixth, 1983; 11th, 1982; *giant slalom:* fourth, 1983; sixth, 1982.

From being European junior downhill champion in 1980, the young Swiss has made rapid strides to become one of the best giant slalom experts in the world. Interestingly, in 1980, he was also Swiss junior champion in the downhill, and second in the slalom. No mention yet of the giant slalom, which is a sort of mid-way point between the other two. After a good start on the 1982 World Cup circuit he really arrived in 1983: third at Val d'Isere, third at Madonna, then a superb victory at Adelboden when he produced a storming second run, 12th at Kranjska Gora, second at Garmisch, third at Todtnau, ninth at Gallivare, eighth at Aspen, 21st at Vail and fifth at Furano. So apart from the disaster at Vail – he was slow on both runs – and Kranjska Gora, he was not out of the top ten.

He lists his hobbies as music and tennis.

Acknowledgements

The information in this book was compiled by **Chris Hilton,** who wishes to thank the following for their help:
Alan Smith, Sandra Stevenson, John Hennessy, Konrad Bartelski, Andy Shaw, Angela Gebhardt, John Moore, Helen Jordan of Peter Stuyvesant, Sherry Daly of the British Bobsleigh Association; the French, Swiss, British, United States Ski Federations; the Novosti Press Agency; the Athletes Information Centre, Ottawa; the London embassies of Switzerland, the German Democratic Republic, the U.S.S.R., the BBC and the International Ski Federation.
Because there are not many reference works on winter sport, we have leant heavily on the excellent *Ski Sunday* book by John Samuel, *Canadian Skater, Ice and Roller Skate, Sport in the G.D.R., Sports Illustrated, Ski Biorama,* the *1983 Canadian Figure Skating Team Guide,* the *Daily Express* (London), *The Sunday Times* (London), *The Guardian* (London), *Ski Survey.*